THE
YOU CAN DO IT!
GUIDE TO
Algebra

Michael J. Goldberger

J. WESTON

WALCH

PUBLISHER

Portland, Maine

For anyone who wants to improve in algebra.

Thank you, Margaret Hastings, for letting me use your computer.

User's Guide
to
Walch Reproducible Books

As part of our general effort to provide educational materials which are as practical and economical as possible, we have designated this publication a "reproducible book." The designation means that purchase of the book includes purchase of the right to limited reproduction of all pages on which this symbol appears:

Here is the basic Walch policy: We grant to individual purchasers of this book the right to make sufficient copies of reproducible pages for use by all students of a single teacher. This permission is limited to a single teacher, and does not apply to entire schools or school systems, so institutions purchasing the book should pass the permission on to a single teacher. Copying of the book or its parts for resale is prohibited.

Any questions regarding this policy or requests to purchase further reproduction rights should be addressed to:

Permissions Editor
J. Weston Walch, Publisher
321 Valley Street • P. O. Box 658
Portland, Maine 04104-0658

1   2   3   4   5   6   7   8   9   10

ISBN 0-8251-2851-X

Copyright © 1996
J. Weston Walch, Publisher
P.O. Box 658 • Portland, Maine 04104-0658

Printed in the United States of America

Contents

Graphing and Solving for x

Graphs of Conic Sections

Square Roots and Logarithms

To the Teacher

Welcome to *The You Can Do It! Guide to Algebra*. This is an algebra help book for students from junior high age to adult. It is 62 sets of step-by-step algebra instructions and problems taken from my tutoring of junior high, high school, and college students. So, it's the cream of hundreds of hours, written down in simple language that everyone can understand.

The book covers the whole smorgasbord of algebra, including factoring, word problems, equations (solving for *x*), square roots, and much more. Each of the 62 sets begins with the important points for the topic and ends with a series of problems for the student to solve.

The book includes a complete answer key, a dictionary for word problems, directions for factoring, and lots of shortcuts, memory devices, and diagrams.

The pages are reproducible, which means you can make as many copies as you need for the students in your classes. And you can present the topics in the order that you wish.

The You Can Do It! Guide to Algebra was written to restore the math student's dignity and to relieve you of some of the pressures of delivering lectures and teaching from textbooks.

The material in this book was at one time offered as a downloadable file on America Online. It received over 2000 downloads and many commendations from users. Students used it to pass courses, and teachers used it to teach students.

In essence, this book is a collection of directions once given to struggling students that focused their minds and helped them solve problems. It helped relieve students of math anxiety and enabled them to get through math. If your students have a problem with factoring, go directly to the pages on factoring. Concentrate only on what they need to focus on. Then make sure they just go slowly and follow the steps!

—Michael J. Goldberger

The Lion's Roar is the fearless proclamation that everything is doable.

—Buddhist saying

Tips

1. Go slowly, step by step. Please focus on only one step at a time.

2. Remember that it is all about understanding. If you *don't* understand it, how can it not be hard? If you *do* understand it, how can it not be easy?

3. You can do it!

4. Find someone who has successfully gone through the class, to give yourself a positive role model to follow.

5. Find a tutor or helpful student who will help you when you need it. If you're stressed or need a lot of help, don't ask close friends or prospective friends to tutor you. Get help from a professional, and keep your friends your friends.

6. Ask questions; that gives you understanding. Use school to your advantage.

7. Do your homework as if you were doing a test. Get in the habit of writing neatly, etc.

8. You can take a class as many times as you need to, which is far superior to cheating.

9. Math is mostly mental exercise, like phys ed for the brain. Remember to detach yourself from the struggle, and remember math's function in your life.

10. If you don't understand something, seek out a better explanation that you *can* understand. Try to rephrase a new concept in terms of something you already understand.

11. Don't spend too much time talking about math with unsympathetic people.

12. There are different levels of math classes. Look for the best class for you. Classes that assign homework help your understanding, because you will have to be more involved.

13. If you have a problem with your teacher, talk to your teacher about it.

General Problems

1. Combining Positive and Negative Numbers

- Every number has a sign, making it either positive or negative. A plus (+) sign may be implied. For example, the number 5 is really positive 5 or +5. The number –1 is negative 1.

- A number can have many plus and/or minus signs preceding it.

- **To tell if a number is positive or negative, count the number of minus signs before a number.** An even (2,4,6,8, etc.) total of minus signs before a number makes the number positive, regardless of the amount of plus signs before it. An odd total (1,3,5,7,9, etc.) of minus signs makes the number negative.

  Examples:

  – – – – 14 (four minus signs make it positive 14.)

  + – + – 6 (two minus signs make it positive 6.)

  + + + – 1 (one minus sign makes it negative 1.)

  + – – – – – 42 (six minus signs makes it positive 42.)

- Parentheses don't affect the counting of minus signs before a number. For example:

  – (– 4) (two minus signs makes it positive 4.)

Step 1: First, identify each number's sign.

  Examples:

  – (– 6) + – 2   (two minus signs before 6 make it positive 6.)
  (one minus sign before 2 makes it negative 2.)

  1 – – + 3   (zero minus signs before 1 make it positive 1.)
  (two minus signs before 3 make it positive 3.)

Step 2: Then combine the numbers.

  To combine two negative numbers: Ignore their signs and add them. Then attach a negative sign to the final answer.

  Example: Combine –2 and –4. Ignore the signs. 2 + 4 = 6. Attach a minus. Answer: –6

To combine one positive and one negative number: Ignore their signs and subtract the lesser number from the greater number. Attach the original sign of the greater number to the final answer.

Example: Combine –8 and 4. Ignore the signs. 8 – 4 = 4. Attach the original sign of the 8 (a minus sign). Answer: –4.

To combine two positive numbers: Add them.

Problems, 1. Combining Positive and Negative Numbers

Combine the following numbers:

1. 3 – – 2

2. 10 + – – – 5

3. – 4 + – – 2

4. + + – – 2 – – + + – – 1

5. + – 6 + – – – –1

2. Moving Terms Across the Equal Sign

- Moving terms means taking a term (number or variable term) and moving it to the opposite side of the equal sign in order to "isolate the variable."

- Every term is either positive (it has a plus sign in front of it, or the plus is implied, e.g., the number 100), or negative (it has a minus sign in front of it).

- When moving a term to the other side, change its sign.

  Examples:

  To move the +2 to the right side of the equal sign, change it to a –2.

  $$3 + 2 = 5$$
  $$3 = 5 - 2$$

  To move the –2 to the right side of the equal sign, change it to a +2.

  $$x - 2 = 5$$
  $$x = 5 + 2$$

  To move the x to the right side of the equal sign, make it a $-x$.

  $$x + y = 2$$
  $$y = 2 - x$$

  To move the $-4y$ to the right side of the equal sign, make it a $+ 4y$.

  $$x - 4y = 12$$
  $$x = 12 + 4y$$

  Move all terms to the right side.

$x + 3a - 3b = 2$	
$x + 3a = 2 + 3b$	(moved the $-3b$ over)
$x = 2 + 3b - 3a$	(moved the $3a$ over)
$0 = 2 + 3b - 3a - x$	(moved the x over)

- Moving terms is a shortcut for adding something to both sides, or subtracting something from both sides.

Problems, 2. Moving Terms Across the Equal Sign

Move the number to the right-hand side of the equation:

1. $x + 2 = 5$

2. $x - 12 = 14$

3. $x - 2 = 6$

4. $x - 2 = 0$

5. $2x + 4y + 1 = 5$

3. A New Way to Do Fractions

No more common denominators!

Fraction Addition

$$\frac{1}{2} + \frac{2}{3}$$

Multiply in a crisscross, and add the results to get the answer numerator.

$$3 \times 1 = \mathbf{3} \qquad 2 \times 2 = \mathbf{4}$$

$$\frac{1}{2} + \frac{2}{3}$$

$$\mathbf{3} + \mathbf{4} = 7$$

Multiply the denominators (bottoms of fractions) across, to get the denominator.

$$\frac{1}{2} + \frac{2}{3} \qquad 2 \times 3 = 6$$

Make the answer fraction.

$$\frac{7}{6}$$

Fraction Subtraction (Go Left to Right)

Do the same steps, except subtract (left to right) the crisscross products.

$$\frac{1}{2} - \frac{1}{3}$$

$$3 \times 1 = \mathbf{3} \qquad 2 \times 1 = \mathbf{2}$$

$$\frac{1}{2} - \frac{1}{3}$$

$$\mathbf{3} - \mathbf{2} = 1$$

Multiply denominators.

$$\frac{1}{2} - \frac{1}{3} \qquad 2 \times 3 = 6$$

Make the answer fraction.

$$\frac{1}{6}$$

This works for all fractions. Always multiply upwards. You may have to reduce the fraction answers.

Problems, 3. A New Way to Do Fractions

Add or subtract the following fractions:

1. $\dfrac{1}{2} + \dfrac{2}{3}$

2. $\dfrac{1}{2} - \dfrac{2}{3}$

3. $\dfrac{1}{3} + \dfrac{1}{4}$

4. $\dfrac{1}{3} - \dfrac{1}{4}$

5. $\dfrac{5}{8} + \dfrac{1}{5}$

4. Reducing Fractions

- You reduce a fraction to get smaller equivalent fractions needed for answers.

- To reduce a fraction, divide the top (numerator) and the bottom (denominator) of the fraction by the same number.

Example:

$$\frac{5}{15}$$

Both top and bottom can be divided by 5.

$$\frac{5 \div 5 = 1}{15 \div 5 = 3}$$

Example:

$$\frac{5 \div 5 = 1}{10 \div 5 = 2} \qquad \frac{5}{10} = \frac{1}{2}$$

Example:

$$\frac{12}{48}$$

$$\frac{12 \div 2 = 6}{48 \div 2 = 24}$$

$$\frac{6 \div 2 = 3}{24 \div 2 = 12}$$

$$\frac{3 \div 3 = 1}{12 \div 3 = 4}$$

$$\text{So } \frac{12}{48} = \frac{1}{4}$$

- Fractions with variables can be reduced, too.

- Subtract equal amounts from the **exponents** of **same letters**.

$$\frac{x^8}{x^5}$$ (Subtract 5 from each x variable's exponent.)

$$\frac{x^3}{x^0}$$ (because $8 - 5 = 3$ and $5 - 5 = 0$)

$$\frac{x^3}{1}$$ (because x^0 equals 1)

$$x^3$$ (because denominators of 1 drop out)

Problems, 4. Reducing Fractions

Reduce each fraction:

1. $\dfrac{2}{6}$

2. $\dfrac{5}{20}$

3. $\dfrac{6}{15}$

4. $\dfrac{x^5}{x^3}$

5. $\dfrac{x^7}{x^1}$

5. Ratio Proportions

Here are some tips for solving typical ratio-proportion problems.

Example:
If 1 pound is 2.2 kilograms, how many kilograms are 12 pounds?

Step 1. There are two "quantities" here: pounds and kilograms. Make the quantities into a fraction:

$$\frac{\text{pounds}}{\text{kilograms}}$$

The first numbers are 1 pound and 2.2 kilograms.

$$\frac{1 \text{ pound}}{2.2 \text{ kilograms}}$$

Notice how the order (pounds in the numerator, kilograms in the denominator) is maintained.

Step 2. Next is 12 pounds and an unknown number of kilograms. Let x stand for the unknown.

$$\frac{12 \text{ pounds}}{x \text{ kilograms}}$$

Step 3. Set the fractions equal.

$$\frac{1 \text{ pound}}{2.2 \text{ kilograms}} = \frac{12 \text{ pounds}}{x \text{ kilograms}}$$

Step 4. Multiply in an upwards crisscross, set the products equal, and solve.

$$1(x) = 1x \qquad 2.2(12) = 26.4$$

$$\frac{1 \text{ pound}}{2.2 \text{ kilograms}} \diagup\!\!\!\!\diagdown \frac{12 \text{ pounds}}{x \text{ kilograms}}$$

$$1x = 26.4$$
$$x = 26.4 \text{ kilograms in 12 pounds}$$

Example:
If a jogger can run a mile in 6 minutes, how many miles can the jogger run in 28 minutes?

Step 1. The two quantities are miles and minutes. Make a fraction.

$$\frac{\text{miles}}{\text{minutes}}$$

The first numbers are 1 mile and 6 minutes.

$$\frac{1 \text{ mile}}{6 \text{ minutes}}$$

Notice how the order (miles in the numerator, minutes in the denominator) is maintained.

(continued)

Step 2. Next is an unknown amount of miles and 28 minutes. Let x stand for the unknown.

$$\frac{x \text{ miles}}{28 \text{ minutes}}$$

Step 3. Set the fractions equal.

$$\frac{1 \text{ mile}}{6 \text{ minutes}} = \frac{x \text{ miles}}{28 \text{ minutes}}$$

Step 4. Cross multiply and divide: Multiply in an upwards crisscross, set the products equal, and solve.

$$\frac{1 \text{ mile}}{6 \text{ minutes}} = \frac{x \text{ miles}}{28 \text{ minutes}}$$

$$28 = 6x$$

$$x = \frac{26}{6} \text{ or } 4\frac{4}{6} \text{ or } 4\frac{2}{3} \text{ or } 4.67 \text{ (miles in 28 minutes)}$$

Note About Calculators and Fractions

Your calculator may have "fraction keys" for doing work with fractions. Check your calculator. If it has an **a b/c** key or a **b/c** key, your calculator can add, multiply, etc., fractions. To enter a fraction into the calculator, enter the numerator, press **a b/c**, and type in the denominator. Then press **+, –,** ×, ÷ depending on the operation being performed. Then enter the second fraction. Press **=**. To enter a mixed-number fraction such as $1\frac{3}{4}$, press **1, a b/c, 3, a b/c, 4**.

Problems, 5. Ratio Proportions

1. If 1 pound is 16 ounces, how many ounces are in 4 pounds?

2. If a worker can assemble a flashlight in 15 minutes, how many flashlights can the worker make in 50 minutes?

3. If a jogger can run a kilometer in 5 minutes, how many kilometers can the jogger run in 38 minutes?

4. If Soupy can eat 10 peanut candies in 4 minutes, how many can he eat in 18 minutes?

5. If Pete makes $7 an hour, how many dollars will he make in $5\frac{1}{2}$ hours?

6. Properties and Identities

Associative Property of Addition and Multiplication

The associative property deals with associations of parentheses. It allows for the parentheses to change what they enclose.

Example of addition: **(2 + 4)** + 12 = 2 + **(4 + 12)**

Example of multiplication: **(2** × **4)** × 12 = 2 × **(4** × **12)**

Commutative Property of Addition and Multiplication

Here, the order of the numbers is what's important. The **Co**mmutative property allows the numbers to **c**hange **o**rder.

Example of addition: 1 + 5 + 7 = 1 + 7 + 5

Example of multiplication: (1 × 5) × 7 = 7 × (1 × 5)

What property is this an example of?

$$(1 + 5) + 7 = 7 + (5 + 1)$$

This is an example of change of order, the commutative property of addition. Notice that the parentheses enclose the "same" thing (1 and 5, added).

The Reflexive Property

Something equals itself.

Example: 2 = 2

The Addition of Zero Identity

If you add 0 to something, it keeps its identity.

Example: 2 + 0 = 2

The Distributive Property

Multiply separately the external number by each number enclosed inside the parentheses.

$$a\,(b + c) = ab + ac$$

Example: 2 (2 + 6) = 2 (2) + 2 (6)

                         4 + 12 = 16

Example: −2 (1 + 2) = −2 (1) + − 2 (2) = −2 + − 4 = − 6

Example: $2x\,(x + 1) = 2x\,(x) + 2x(1) = 2x^2 + 2x$

The Zero Identity of Multiplication

Anything times 0 = 0.

Example: 10 × 0 = 0.

Problems, 6. Properties and Identities

Name the property in each equation:

1. $(1 + 3) + 2 = 1 + (3 + 2)$

2. $1 + (3 + 2) = (3 + 2) + 1$

3. $3 (2 + 1) = 3 (2) + 3 (1)$

4. $2 + 0 = 2$

5. $3 \times 2 \times 1 = 1 \times 2 \times 3$

7. FOIL Method

Use the FOIL method to multiply two parentheses. To use the FOIL method, you multiply **F**irsts, **O**utsides, **I**nsides, and **L**asts.

In two parentheses, these positions are

Firsts: $(x\quad)\quad(x\quad)$

Outsides: $(x\quad)\quad(\quad x)$

Insides: $(\quad x)\quad(x\quad)$

Lasts: $(\quad x)\quad(\quad x)$ The "lasts" have important signs, too.

Example: Multiply (1 + **4**) (2 + **3**) using the FOIL method.

Firsts: $(1) \times (2) = 2$

Outsides: $(1) \times (+3) = +3$

Insides: $(+4) \times (2) = +8$

Lasts: $(+4) \times (+3) = +12$

Writing them out as a list: 2 + 3 + 8 + 12 = 25.

Example with variables: Multiply (x + **2**) (x − **3**)

Firsts: $(x) \times (x) = x^2$

Outsides: $(x) \times (-3) = -3x$

Insides: $(+2) \times (x) = +2x$

Lasts: $(+2) \times (-3) = -6$

$-3x$ and $+2x$ are like terms and can be combined

Writing them out as a list: $x^2 - 3x + 2x - 6 = x^2 - 1x - 6$.

• Watch for signs: A negative number multiplied by a negative number equals a positive number.

• If terms are composed of more than one letter (like $2xy$, for example), write the letters in alphabetical order.

• Be on the lookout for squared parentheses, such as $(x + 2)^2$.

The FOIL method should be used because they are multiplication problems: $(x + 2)^2 = (x + 2)(x + 2)$.

Problems, 7. FOIL Method

Use the FOIL method to multiply the following:

1. $(x + 3)(x + 4)$

2. $(x + 2)(x + 6)$

3. $(x + 3)(x - 2)$

4. $(x + 10)(x - 4)$

5. $(x - 4)(x - 3)$

8. Absolute Value

Did you know that absolute value means "the distance from zero on the number line?" On the number line below, there are dots at –4 and at 4; both have the same distance from 0—that is, four units of distance. Distance from zero is always a positive number, or at minimum, zero.

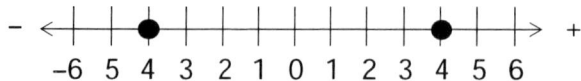

-6 5 4 3 2 1 0 1 2 3 4 5 6

Thus we say the absolute value of –4 is 4 (units from zero) and the absolute value of 4 is 4, too. Absolute value is written with bars, so the absolute value of –4 is written like this: $|-4|$. The absolute value of 4 is written like this: $|4|$. Both equal 4 (units from zero).

What is the absolute value of 3, written $|3|$? It's 3 (units from zero).
What is the absolute value of –3, written $|-3|$? It's 3 (units from zero).

These are three kinds of absolute-value problems:

The Equals Case	**The Less-than Case**	**The Greater-than Case**
|something| = some other	|something| < some other |something| ≤ some other	|something| > some other |something| ≥ some other
The answer will look like: $x = 3, 4$	The answer will look like: $x < 8$ and $x > 1$	The answer will look like: $x < -2$ or $x > 4$

A way of remembering this is that the less-than problem gives you an "in-between" graph answer. The ≤ looks like the < case, while the ≥ looks like the > case; but use **closed** dots for their graphs.

Solving Absolute-Value Problems

Follow these steps for almost all absolute-value problems.

Step 1. Make two columns.

Step 2. In the left column, rewrite the problem exactly, except without absolute-value bars.

Step 3. In the right column, rewrite the problem, but with no absolute-value bars. Also, change the direction of the sign: > becomes <, < becomes >, and = remains =. Put the right side of the equation into a parentheses and multiply it times (–1).

(continued)

Step 4. Solve both columns. You will get two solutions. Graph according to the examples above.

A Greater-than Case

Example: $|x + 2| > 5$

$x + 2 > 5$
$x > 5 - 2$
$x > 3$

$x + 2 < (-1)(5)$
$x + 2 < -5$
$x < -5 - 2$
$x < -7$

To express: arrows face right, and say "or." $-7 > x$ or $x > 3$. Low   High

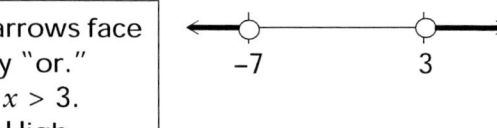

-7 3

A Less-than Case

Example: $|x + 2| < 6$

$x + 2 < 6$
$x < 6 - 2$
$x < 4$

$x + 2 > (-1)(6)$
$x + 2 > -6$
$x > -6 - 2$
$x > -8$

To express: arrows face left. $-8 < x < 4$. Low   High "**Less** than points **Left**."

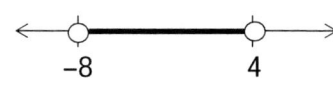

-8 4

Problems, 8. Absolute Value

Solve and graph the following absolute-value problems.

1. $|x + 4| > 1$

2. $|x + 1| < 2$

3. $|x + 4| = 6$

4. $|x - 7| > 3$

5. $|x + 5| < 8$

9. Synthetic Division

In a division problem with variables, the terms you divide by may be in one of these forms:

$$(x + \text{number}) \quad \text{or} \quad (x - \text{number})$$

You can shorten your work by doing division the "synthetic" way:

Example: $x^4 - 2x^3 + 4x^2 + 6 \div (x + 3)$ is suitable for synthetic division because the divisor is $(x + 3)$.

Here is how to divide the following:

Example: $x^2 + 7x - 8 \div (x - 1)$

Coefficient of x^2 is +1 (implied).
Coefficient of $+7x$ is +7.
Coefficient of -8 is -8.

Step 1. Write the dividend's $(x^2 + 7x - 8)$ coefficients in a row, leaving space. Leave some space below this row and draw a line.

$$1 \quad 7 \quad -8$$

> *Note:* A divisor like $x^2 + 8$ should be rewritten as $x^2 + 0x + 8$; here, variables must decline in powers by steps of 1. Put in $+0$ (the variable).

Step 2. Put the opposite of the divisor's $(x - 1)$ number (the opposite of -1 is 1) in a box below and to the left of the coefficients.

$$\boxed{1} \quad 1 \quad 7 \quad -8$$

Step 3. Bring the first coefficient below the line. Multiply the box times the number below the line, and put the product above the line in the second column.

$$\boxed{1} \quad \begin{array}{ccc} 1 & 7 & -8 \\ & 1 & \\ \hline 1 & & \end{array}$$

1×1 (in the box) = 1 above line

Step 4. Add the second column, putting the sum (with its sign) below the line.

$$\boxed{1} \quad \begin{array}{ccc} 1 & 7 & -8 \\ & 1 & \\ \hline 1 & +8 & \end{array}$$

$7 + 1 = 8$ below the line.

Step 5. Multiply times the box, put the sum in the third column, then add down.

$$\boxed{1} \quad \begin{array}{ccc} 1 & 7 & -8 \\ & 1 & 8 \\ \hline 1 & +8 & +0 \end{array}$$

8×1 (in the box) = 8 above line.

(continued)

- Take the dividend's **variables only** (which are x^2 and x).

- Skip over the variable with the greatest number exponent (here the x^2).

- Associate (in order) the remaining variables with the numbers below the line.

- The last number below the line is always the "remainder" if there is one. $1(x) + 8$ (no variable) $+ 0$ (no remainder). Answer: $1x + 8$, R(emainder) 0.

Problems, 9. Synthetic Division

1. $(3x^2 + 6x + 3) \div (x + 1)$

2. $(2x^2 + 9x + 10) \div (x + 2)$

3. $(x^2 + x - 12) \div (x - 3)$

4. $(5x^2 + 21x + 4) \div (x + 4)$

5. $(4x^2 + 3x - 7) \div (x - 1)$

Factoring

10. Common Factoring: Numbers

The first step in common factoring is to find the greatest number that can divide cleanly (with no remainder) into a series of numbers.

- What's the greatest number that divides cleanly into these numbers?
  | 6 | 12 | 24 |

  Answer: 6

- The greatest number that divides cleanly into these numbers is 4:
  | 24 | 20 | 12 |

- The greatest number that divides cleanly into these numbers is 5:
  | 25 | 30 | 35 |

- The greatest number that divides cleanly into these numbers is 10:
  | 30 | 20 | 10 |

Now that we understand this process, we can complete the steps in common factoring.

Factor: 6 + 12 + 24

Step 1. Find the greatest number that can divide cleanly into 6, 12, and 24.

Step 2. Put this greatest number (here, 6) on the outside of spacious parentheses.

6 (   )

Step 3. Divide each number in the problem by 6. Put the results (carrying over the signs) inside the parentheses.

$$6 + 12 + 24$$

Becomes   6 (1 + 2 + 4)

$6 \div 6 = 1$
$12 \div 6 = 2$
$24 \div 6 = 4$

Example:

Factor: 20 + 30 + 50

The greatest number that divides cleanly is 10.

$$20 + 30 + 50$$
$$10 (2 + 3 + 5)$$

$20 \div 10 = 2$
$30 \div 10 = 3$
$50 \div 10 = 5$

Example:

20 + 30 – 5

The greatest number that divides cleanly is 5.

$$20 + 30 - 5$$
$$5 (4 + 6 - 1)$$

$20 \div 5 = 4$
$30 \div 5 = 6$
$5 \div 5 = 1$

Problems, 10. Common Factoring: Numbers

Factor:

1. 2 + 6 + 10

2. 4 + 12 + 20

3. 15 + 10 – 25

4. 16 + 24 – 4

5. –21 + 28 – 14

11. Common Factoring: Variables

Follow these steps to factor terms with variables:

Step 1. To factor out common variables, find the common letter that is in all the terms. Find the letter's lowest power occurrence.

Problem: $x^2 + x^4 - x^6$

- What is the common letter to all these terms? What is this letter's lowest power?

The common letter is x, and x^2 is its lowest power occurrence.

Step 2. Write this outside of spacious parentheses.

Problem: $x^2 + x^4 - x^6$

Common Factor: x^2 ( )

Step 3. Subtract 2 (because x^2 is the lowest power occurrence of the common letter x) from each x exponent in the original problem. Put the results (with the signs) inside the parentheses.

Problem: $x^2 + x^4 - x^6$

Factored: $x^2 (x^0 + x^2 - x^4)$

Follow these steps to factor terms with more than one common variable:

Step 1. Find the common letters and their lowest powers.

Problem: $x^3y^5 + x^4y^7 - x^6y^4$

x and y are common to each term. Their lowest powers are x^3 and y^4.

Step 2. Write the lowest power occurrences in alphabetical order outside of spacious parentheses.

Problem: $x^3y^6 + x^4y^5 - x^6y^4$

Common Factor: x^3y^4 ( )

Step 3. Subtract 3 from the problem's x-variable exponents. Subtract 4 from the y-variable exponents. Put the results (and the signs) in the parentheses.

Problem: $x^3y^6 + x^4y^5 - x^6y^4$

Factored: $x^3y^4 (x^0y^2 + x^1y^1 - x^3y^0)$

Any letter raised to the power of 0 turns into 1, because anything raised to the 0 power equals a whole number of 1.

Factored: $x^3y^4 (x^0y^2 + x^1y^1 - x^3y^0)$

Now: $x^3y^4 (1y^2 + x^1y^1 - 1x^3)$

The You Can Do It! Guide to Algebra

Problems, 11. Common Factoring: Variables

Factor:

1. $x + x^3$

2. $x^4 + x^2$

3. $x^2y^2 - x^1y^3$

4. $x^2y^2z^2 + x^4y^3z$

5. $a^2bc + 2ab + 3ac$

12. Common Factoring: Numbers and Variables

When you factor numbers and variables (letters) at the same time, you still work the problem as though you were doing the two steps separately.

Step 1. Factor the numbers.

Problem: $4x^3 + 8x^5 - 6x^4$

Just numbers (with signs): $4 + 8 - 6$

The greatest number that divides cleanly into all the numbers is 2.
Numbers: $4 + 8 - 6$
Factored: $2 (2 + 4 - 3)$

Step 2. Factor the variables.

Variables (no signs): $x^3 \ x^5 \ x^4$

The common letter is x, and its lowest power occurrence is x^3.
$$x^3 \ x^5 \ x^4$$
$$x^3 (x^0 \ x^2 \ x^1)$$

Step 3. Put the answer together.

Combine the answers of the numbers factoring and the variables factoring. Write the numbers in front of the variables.

Numbers (with signs): $2 (2 + 4 - 3)$
Variables (letters): $x^3 (x^0 \ x^2 \ x^1)$
Combined for answer: $2x^3 (2x^0 + 4x^2 - 3x^1)$

Here is another example:

Problem: $2x^2y^4 + 4x^1y^2$

Just numbers (with signs): $2 + 4$
Factored: $2 (1 + 2)$

Just variables: $x^2y^4 + x^1y^2$
Factored: $x^1y^2 (x^1y^2 + x^0y^0)$

Numbers answer: $2 (1 + 2)$
Variables answer: $x^1y^2 (x^1y^2 + x^0y^0)$
Combined: $2x^1y^2 (1x^1y^2 + 2x^0y^0)$
$2x^1y^2 (1x^1y^2 + 2 (1) (1))$
$2x^1y^2 (1x^1y^2 + 2)$

Problems, 12. Common Factoring: Numbers and Variables

Factor:

1. $2x^2 + 4x^5$

2. $14x^3 + 18x^{12}$

3. $5x^2y^2 - 10x^1y^3$

4. $3x^2y^2 + 9x^4y^3$

5. $12x^1y^2 + 6x^1y^3$

13. Factoring: Three Terms

To use this factoring method:

- Three terms (an x^2 term, an x term, and a number term) are required.

- Coefficients are numbers that precede a letter, or are numbers that stand alone.

- The x^2 term must have an implied or actual coefficient of +1.

x^2 is the x^2 term. $\underline{x^2 + 3x}\,(+ 2)$ +1 (implied) is the coefficient of x^2.
+3x is the x term   +3 is the coefficient of x.
+2 is the number term.   +2 is the coefficient of +2.

Step 1. Identify the number term (here, the +2). Make multiplication pairs: Write down all positive, negative, and one positive/one negative pairs of multiplication factors whose product makes this number.

Multiplication pairs that make +2

$$+2 \times +1$$
$$-2 \times -1$$

Step 2. Add the numbers, going across.

$$\boxed{+2 + +1} = \left(+3\right)$$
$$-2 + -1 = -3$$

Put a box around the pair whose sum is equal to the x term's coefficient (here, +3).

Step 3. Make two spacious parentheses, next to each other.

$$(\qquad)\ (\qquad)$$

Put the boxed pair numbers (and their signs) into the right-hand sides of the parentheses.

$$(\qquad + 2)\ (\qquad + 1)$$

Step 4. Split the x^2 term into "halves" of x and x. Put these into the left-hand sides of the parentheses.

$$(x^1 + 2)\ (x^1 + 1)$$

You don't have to write x^1s. $(x + 2)\ (x + 1)$

Step 5. If you multiply these two parentheses out using the FOIL method, you will get the original problem again.

(continued)

Here is another example:

x^2 is the x^2 term.　　　$\underline{x^2}\ \underline{-5x}\ \underline{+\ 4}$　　　+1 implied if the coefficient of x.
$-5x$ is the x term.　　　　　　　　　　　　　　-5 is the coefficient of x.
$+4$ is the number term.　　　　　　　　　　　$+4$ is the coefficient of $+4$.

Step 1. Make multiplication pairs for +4 (the number term).

Step 2. Add the factor pairs. Put a box around the pair whose sum is the coefficient of x (here, −5).

Multiplication pairs that make +4	**Sums of these pairs**
$+4 \times +1$	$+4 + +1 = +5$
-4×-1	$\boxed{-4 + -1} = \widehat{(-5)}$
$+2 \times +2$	$+2 + +2 = +4$
-2×-2	$-2 + -2 = -4$

Step 3. Put the boxed numbers into parentheses.

$$(\quad\ -4\ )\ (\quad\ -1\ )$$

Step 4. Split the x^2 term into "halves" of x^1 and x^1 and put these in the left-hand sides of the parentheses. You don't have to write powers of 1:
$(\ x-4\ )\ (\ x-1\ )$

Step 5. If you multiply these two parentheses out using the FOIL method, you will get the original problem again.

　　　　　　　　　　The You Can Do It! Guide to Algebra

Problems, 13. Factoring: Three Terms

Factor:

1. $x^2 + 5x + 4$

2. $x^2 + 7x + 12$

3. $x^2 + 4x + 4$

4. $x^2 - 5x + 6$

5. $x^2 + 1x - 6$

14. Factoring: Two Terms, Difference of Squares

This factoring method requires the following:

- There must be two terms and a minus sign (*Example:* $x^2 - 9$).

- The numbers or variables must be perfect squares. A perfect square is a value formed by multiplying something times itself.

Examples:

1 (1 = 1×1) , 4 (4 = 2×2), 9 (9 = 3×3), 16, 25, 36, 49, 64, 81, 100, 121, 144, 169

Also $x^2 = x \times x$, $x^4 = x^2 \times x^2$, $x^6 = x^3 \times x^3$, and $x^{\text{even number}} = x^{\text{half}} \times x^{\text{half}}$

Step 1. Identify perfect squares.

Example: $x^2 - 9$

- They are both perfect squares.

- Split the perfect squares into their two multiplication pieces.

- Here, x^2 splits into $x^1 \times x^1$, and 9 splits into 3×3.

Step 2. Put the "pieces" into the left and right sides of two sets of parentheses.

$$x^2 - 9 \qquad\qquad x^2 - 9$$

$$(x^1 \qquad) \ (x^1 \qquad) \quad (\qquad 3) \ (\qquad 3)$$

Together: $\qquad (x^1 \quad 3) \ (x^1 \quad 3)$

Step 3. Put a plus in the middle of one parentheses and a minus in the other.

$$(x^1 + 3) \ (x^1 - 3)$$

Here is another example: $\qquad 25x^4 - 49y^6$

- There are two terms separated by a minus sign.

Step 1. Identify perfect squares.

- $25 = 5 \times 5$; $49 = 7 \times 7$
- $x^4 = x^2 \times x^2$
- $y^6 = y^3 \times y^3$

Step 2. Put pieces into parentheses.

$$25x^4 \qquad\qquad\qquad 49y^6$$

$$(5x^2 \qquad) \ (5x^2 \qquad) \quad (\qquad 7y^3) \ (\qquad 7y^3)$$

Together: $\qquad (5x^2 \quad 7y^3) \ (5x^2 \quad 7y^3)$

Step 3. Add plus and minus signs: $(5x^2 + 7y^3) \ (5x^2 - 7y^3)$

The You Can Do It! Guide to Algebra

Problems, 14. Factoring: Two Terms, Difference of Squares

Factor:

1. $x^2 - 16$

2. $x^2 - 25$

3. $x^6 - y^2$

4. $4x^2 - 25y^6$

5. $y^4 - 81$

15. Factoring: Trial and Error Factoring

This factoring method works when the coefficient of (the number that precedes) x^2 is anything other than +1, and the terms cannot be factored out through common factoring.

$2x$ is the x^2 term. $+7x$ is the x term. $+3$ is the number term.	$2x^2 + 7x + 3$	2 is the x^2 term's coefficient. $+7$ is the x term's coefficient. $+3$ is the number term's coefficient.

Step 1. Make all multiplication factor pairs for the leftmost and rightmost coefficients, as shown:

$$2x^2 + 7x + 3$$

can be 2 × 1   can be +3 × +1

–2 × –1   –3 × –1

Step 2. Make two parentheses and put a pair of factors from the x^2 term into the left-hand sides of the parentheses. Put a pair of factors from the number term into the right-hand side of the parentheses.

Trying 2 × 1 and +3 × +1
   (2 + 3) (1 + 1)

- If all three coefficients are positive, then put in only positive pairs of factors, such as 7 × 2.

- If **the number term is negative, and** the coefficient of the x term is negative, the second pair's should be one with a negative factor "larger" than the positive factor, such as –7 × 2.

- **If the number is negative, but** the coefficient of the x term is positive, the second set of factors should have a "larger" positive number than negative number, such as 7 × –2.

Here, since all coefficients are positive, try only positive pairs. Cross out negative pairs. $2x^2 + 7x + 3$
          can be 2 × 1   can be +3 × +1

         ~~–2 × –1~~   ~~–3 × –1~~

So again, trying 2 × 1 and +3 × +1,
   (2 + 3) (1 + 1)

Do the OI (outside, inside) part of FOIL, and check if the result equals the middle term's coefficient (+7). OI of FOIL: 2 (+1) = +2 ; (+3) (1) = +3; +2 and +3 make +5, which is not +7.

- Rearrange the right-hand pair and try again.

       (2   + 1) (1   + 3)

(continued)

OI of FOIL: 2 (+3) = +6; (+1) (1) = +1; +6 and +1 = +7. +7 does = +7. If not, we would rearrange the left-hand pair or try a new pair combination. To make the final answer, put in x's after the left-hand numbers; move signs to the middle.

$$(2x + 1) \quad (1x + 3)$$

Problems, 15. Factoring: Trial and Error Factoring

Factor:

1. $2x^2 + 5x + 3$

2. $2x^2 + 15x + 7$

3. $3x^2 + 11x + 6$

4. $2x^2 + 3x - 2$

5. $5x^2 + 7x + 2$

16. Factoring, Part I: The AC Coefficient Method

A factoring problem may have **three terms** and a number ≠ 1 (which you can't common factor out) in front of the x^2. In this situation, you're faced with doing "trial and error" two-parentheses factoring or using the no-guesswork "AC method." The AC method, explained below, uses the coefficients of an expression.

$$2x^2 + 9x + 4 \qquad \text{There's a 2 in front of the } x^2.$$

Step 1. Write the coefficients (and their signs) of the terms.

A = The coefficient of the x^2 term.
B = The coefficient of the x term.
C = The number term.

$2x^2 + 9x + 4$
A = + 2
B = + 9
C = + 4

Step 2. Multiply A times C. Write the answer down.

In the example, A is +2 and C is +4.
$$+2 \times + 4 = +8$$

Step 3. Write down all pairs of multiplication factors that multiply to make the number.

$$
\begin{array}{lll}
8 = +1 \times +8 & & +1 + +8 = 9 \\
 = +2 \times +4 & \xrightarrow{\text{Add the factor pairs.}} & +2 + +4 = 6 \\
 = -1 \times -8 & & -1 + -8 = -9 \\
 = -2 \times -4 & & -2 + -4 = -6 \\
\end{array}
$$

Step 4. Add each group of two numbers as shown in the right column above. Take the numbers that make B. Here, B is +9 (see Step 1).
$$+1 \text{ and } +8$$

Step 5. Rewrite the problem, but break the "B" term ($9x$) into two terms using the numbers from Step 4 (here, +1 and +8. The variable x "gets distributed" to the +1 and the +8).

$$2x^2 + 9x + 4$$
$$2x^2 + 1x + 8x + 4$$

Step 6. Factor by grouping to get the answer (instructions on page 36).

$$2x^2 + 1x + 8x + 4$$

$2x^2 + 1x$ $+ 8x + 4$
$x (2x + 1)$ $+ 4 (2x + 1)$

Answer: $(x + 4)(2x + 1)$

(continued)

The first ( ) is composed of the common factors, and the second ( ) is composed of one of the recurring parentheses factors.

Problems, 16. Factoring, Part I: The AC Coefficient Method

Use the AC method to factor the following:

1. $2x^2 + 5x + 3$

2. $2x^2 + 11x + 12$

3. $2x^2 + 7x + 5$

4. $3x^2 + 7x + 2$

5. $2x^2 + 1x - 1$

17. Factoring, Part II: Factoring by Grouping

Prerequisite: Factoring Part I: The AC Coefficient Method, page 34.

Factor by grouping only if there are four or a higher even number of terms.

Step 1. "Group" two terms at a time and common factor each group.

Example: (See Part I.)

$$2x^2 + 1x + 8x + 4 \quad \text{The expression has four terms.}$$

1st group 2nd group Two groups of two terms.

Step 2. Factor each group separately.

$$2x^2 + 1x \qquad\qquad + 8x + 4$$

Greatest common factor: 1	Greatest common factor: 4
Common letter, lowest power: x^1 (or x)	Common letter, lowest power: none
Combined common factor: $1x$	Combined common factor: $+4$ (keep sign)
$2x + 1x$	$+8x + 4$
$1x\,(2x + 1)$	$+4\,(2x + 1)$
Notice that $(2x + 1)$ appears in both factorings.	Notice that you need to factor out a sign from the second group, as it is used in the final answer.

Step 3. Make an answer out of the factored-out common factors and one of the recurring parentheses.

$$(1x + 4) \quad (2x + 1)$$

The first parentheses contain the factored-out common factors from each group. The second parentheses contain one of the recurring factors (here, $2x + 1$).

$$2x^2 + 6x + 3x + 9$$

1st Group: $2x^2 + 6x$	2nd Group: $+3x + 9$
Greatest common factor: 2	Greatest common factor: $+3$
Common letter, lowest power: x	Common letter: none
Combined factor: $2x$	Combined factor: $+3$
Original: $2x^2 + 6x$	Original: $+3x + 9$
Factored: $2x\,(x + 3)$	Factored: $+3\,(x + 3)$

$$(2x + 3)\,(x + 3)$$

The answer is composed of the factors $2x$ and $+3$, and of one of the $(x + 3)$'s.

Problems, 17. Factoring, Part II: Factoring by Grouping

Factor the following by grouping:

1. $x^2 + 7x + 2x + 14$

2. $x^2 + 5x + 4x + 20$

3. $x^2 + 10x + 2x + 20$

4. $3x^2 + 1x + 6x + 2$

5. $2x^2 + 4x - 1x - 2$

18. Factoring: Two Terms, Difference of Cubes

"Difference of cubes" factoring requires two "perfect cube terms" with a minus sign or plus sign in between them.

$$x^3 - 8$$

Perfect cubes are terms formed by multiplying three identical numbers and/or variables (letters) together.

- The number 8 is a perfect cube because it can be formed by multiplying $2 \times 2 \times 2$.

- x^3 is a perfect cube, as it is formed by $x \times x \times x$.

Examples of perfect cubes and their components:

Perfect cube	Cube formed from	Perfect cube	Cube formed from
1	1	x^3	x^1
8	2	x^6	x^2
27	3	x^9	x^3
64	4	$x^3 y^3$	$x^1 y^1$
125	5	Remember: Multiplying variables	
216	6	means adding the powers.	

A perfect cube can be a combination of a number and a variable.

Example: $27x^6$, which is formed by $3x^2 \times 3x^2 \times 3x^2$.

Problems will give you two perfect cubes with a sign in between. You will be asked to find out what the "cube-forming component" was before the "cubing" multiplications.

Follow these steps to factor the following: $8 + x^9$

Step 1. Find the "cube formers."

The first cube former is 2 $(2 \times 2 \times 2 = 8)$; the second "cube former" is x^3.

Step 2. Apply these formulas once you have the first and second cube formers.

Formula, sign is +: $(1st + 2nd) (1st^2 - [1st \times 2nd] + 2nd^2)$
Formula, sign is –: $(1st - 2nd) (1st^2 + [1st \times 2nd] + 2nd^2)$

A memory device: The sign is the formula's first sign, then its opposite, then +. *Example:* If it's the + sign formula, it goes +, –, +. Minus sign formula: –, +, +.

Example: $8 + x^9$ ⟶ First is 2, second is x^3.
Use the + formula

Answer: $(2 + x^3) ((2)^2 - [2 \times x^3] + (x^3)^2)$
$(2 + x^3) (4 - 2x^3 + x^6)$

(continued)

Example: $8x^3 - 27$ ⎯⎯⎯⎯→ First is $2x$, second is 3
                                   Use the – formula
Answer: $(2x - 3) ((2x)^2 + [2x \times 3] + (3)^2)$ $(2x)^2 = (2x) \times (2x)$

                 $(2x - 3) (4x^2 + 6x + 9)$

Problems, 18. Factoring: Two Terms, Difference of Cubes

Factor:

1. $x^3 - 64$

2. $125 + x^3$

3. $216 - x^6$

4. $x^3 - 125$

5. $27 + y^9$

19. Greatest Common Number: Factoring Tips

A number is divisible by

2   . . . if the number ends in 0, 2, 4, 6, or 8
Examples: 12, 14, 62, etc.

3   . . . if the sum of the digits is divisible by 3
Example: 27 = 2 + 7 = 9. 9 is divisible by 3.

4   . . . if the last two digits (taken as a whole) are divisible by 4.
Example: 416. Last two digits = 16. 16 is divisible by 4.

5   . . . if the number ends in 0 or 5.
Examples: 155, 260, etc.

6   . . . if the number is divisible by both 2 and 3.
Example: 624. It divisible by 2, and 6 + 2 + 4 = 12, which is divisible by 3.

8   . . . if the last three digits (taken as a whole) are divisible by 8.
Example: 5016. Last three digits = 016. 16 is divisible by 8.

9   . . . if the sum of the digits is divisible by 9.
Example: 981 = 9 + 8 + 1 = 18, which is divisible by 9.

10   . . . if the number ends in 0.
Example: 152430

12   . . . if the number is divisible by both 3 and 4.
Example: 36. It is divisible by 2. 3 + 6 = 9, which is divisible by 3.

14   . . . if the number is divisible by 2 and 7.
Example: 28. It is divisible by 2, and it is divisible by 7.

15   . . . if the number is divisible by 3 and 5.
Example: 45. It is divisible by 5. 4 + 5 = 9, which is divisible by 3.

Problems, 19. Greatest Common Number: Factoring Tips

Answer the following:

1. Is 726 divisible by 3? how about 721?

2. Is 324 divisible by 9? how about 5256?

3. Is 324 divisible by 4? by 8?

4. Since 16 is divisible by 4, is 116 divisible by 4? is 216? how about 5016?

5. What positive numbers greater than 1 and less than 10 is 320 divisible by?

Word Problems

20. Dictionary for Word Problems

Translations of word problem words into algebra symbols.

a number, the number	x
an amount, an unknown amount	x
the same amount	x and x
twice a number	$2x$
three times a number	$3x$
ten times a number	$10x$
increased by	$+$
more than	$+$
plus	$+$
added to	$+$
the sum	something + something
the difference	something − something
decreased by	−
fewer	−
less, less than	−
subtracted from	−
of, times, multiplied by	×
the product	something × something
the quotient of	something ÷ something
divided by	÷
is, was, will be	=
equals, is equivalent to	=
is not equal to	≠
plus or minus	±
two consecutive integers	$x, x + 1$
two consecutive even integers	$x, x + 2$
two consecutive odd integers	$x, x + 2$
three consecutive integers	$x, x + 1, x + 2$
three consecutive even integers	$x, x + 2, x + 4$
three consecutive odd integers	$x, x + 2, x + 4$
the square of a number	x^2
the cube of a number	x^3
the square root of a number	$\sqrt{x}$
half of a number	$.5x$
the perimeter of a rectangle	Perimeter = Length + Length + Width + Width
the area of a rectangle	Area = Length × Width

The You Can Do It! Guide to Algebra

the perimeter of any shape	Perimeter = Add up all the sides
the area of a square	Area = Side × Side
10 percent (10 per-"cents")	.10 (think of "cents" on a store receipt)
2 percent (2 per-"cents")	.02 (think of 2 cents on a store receipt)
percent	divided by 100

Problems, 20. *Dictionary for Word Problems*

Use algebra symbols to write the following:

1. Eight times a number plus three

2. The square root of a number, less 5

3. The perimeter of a rectangle with lengths of 2 and widths of 4

4. Forty percent

5. Five is equal to three increased by two

21. Word Problems: Age Problems

To solve age problems, translate words into math symbols. For example, the introductory sentence may state: "John is five years older than Martha."

The introductory sentence math key words "older than" translate to the math symbol +. Common math key words and their symbols are:

older than . . .   +
younger than . . .   –
decreased by, less . . .   –
increased by, more, plus   +
twice as old as, three times as old as $2x$, $3x$

Step 1. Find what each person's name equals in math symbols.

   • Underline "is," all key words, all numbers, and all names.

   • The name after <u>is,</u> towards the close of the sentence, equals x.

   • The other name always equals x plus the number, or x minus the number, except when the key words "two times" or "twice as old as" appear. In this case, the other name equals $2x$, or $2x$ plus the number, or $2x$ minus the number, etc.

   Example: <u>Brian is four</u> years <u>older than Michelle.</u>
   Michelle = x (Michelle's name is at the sentence close, after the word "is.")
   From the key, "older than" means "+", and the number is 4, so Brian = $x + 4$.

   Example: <u>Ernie is twice as old</u> as <u>Bert</u>.
   Bert = x (Bert's name is after "is", at the sentence close.)
   "Twice as old" means $2x$, and that's it for key words. Ernie equals $2x$.

   Example: <u>Jeff is 50</u> years <u>younger than Edward.</u>
   Edward = x (Edward's name comes at the sentence end, after the word "is.")
   The key words "younger than" mean "–," and the number is 50, so Jeff = $x - 50$.

   Example: Frank is <u>three times as old</u> as Ernest, <u>less seven</u> years.
   Ernest = x (Ernest comes after the word "is," near the closing words.)
   "Three times as old as" means $3x$, "less" means "–," the number is 7, so Frank = $3x - 7$.

(continued)

Step 2. Translate the second sentence into its equation, and solve.

Wordings	*Equation*
"The sum of their ages is . . ."	(Name 1) + (Name 2) = .
"The difference of their ages is . . ."	(Older person's name) – (Younger person's name) =
"The product of their ages is . . ."	(Name 1) × (Name 2) =
"Twice the older's age is the younger less three ..."	2 (Older's person's name) = (Younger) – 3.

Example: The sum of Brian and Michelle's ages is 44. (Get information from the first example in Step 1.)

(Name 1) + (Name 2) = 44
(Brian) + (Michelle) = 44
$(x + 4) + (x) = 44$
$x + 4 + x = 44$ Michelle is (x), so she is (20).
$2x + 4 = 44$ . . .   Brian is $(x + 4)$, so he is $(20 + 4)$
$2x = 40$ . . . $x = 20$ . . .   = 24.

Problems, 21. Word Problems: Age Problems

Rewrite in math form:

1. Michael is two years younger than Jill.

2. The sum of Dave and Mike's ages is 54.

3. The difference of Dave and Mike's ages is 0.

4. The product of Dave and Shep's ages is 21.

5. Twice Dave's age plus Mike's age is 84.

22. Word Problems: Age Problems in the Future or Past

In age problems, the sentence following the introductory sentence may indicate future or past:

"Five years from now . . ."
"Ten years ago . . ."
"In 20 years . . ."

Follow these steps to solve age problems in the future or past:

Step 1. Put the names into two columns.

- Add or subtract **to or from both columns** the number of years in the future or in the past.

  Future   + (Add the time change to each column.)
  Past   – (Subtract the time change from each column.)

Example: Ten years from now, Michelle will be . . .

(Michelle)	(Brian)
(Michelle + 10)	(Brian + 10)

Step 2. Make the equation with the new row of "time-adjusted" names.

Example: Ten years from now, the <u>sum</u> of their ages <u>will be 64</u>.

(Michelle + 10) + (Brian + 10) = 64
(x + 10) + (<u>x + 4</u> + 10) = 64
x + 10 + x + 4 + 10 = 64
$2x$ + 24 = 64
$2x$ = 40
x = 20 (Michelle is 20. Brian is (20) + 4 = 24.)
In 10 years, Michelle will be 30. Brian will be 34.

Example: <u>Sixteen years ago, Brian was twice Michelle's</u> age.

(Michelle)	(Brian)
(Michelle – 16)	(Brian – 16)

- If the problem is not a "sum" or "difference," then set up the equation as before, except use "time-adjusted" names.

(continued)

Brian was twice Michelle's age.   ("was" means =)

(Brian – 16)   = 2 (Michelle – 16)
($x + 4 - 16$)   = 2 ($x - 16$)
($x - 12$)   = $2x - 32$
$-12 + 32$ = $2x - x$
20 = x

Michelle is 20, Brian is (20) + 4 = 24
Sixteen years ago, Michelle was 4 and Brian was 8.

Problems, 22. Word Problems: Age Problems in the Future or Past

Rewrite in mathematical form:

1. Ten years ago, Mike was three times Bert's age.

2. Five years from now, Ernie will be twice Pete's age.

3. Eight years from now, the sum of Mike and Pele's ages will be 47.

4. Twenty-five years ago, Jill was double Mike's age.

5. In two years, Pele will be Mike's age minus 23.

23. Word Problems with Shapes and Dimensions

Do shape and dimension problems the same way as age problems, using length and width instead of names.

Step 1. Read the first sentence. Define length and width.

- The word "length" or "width" after the word "is," near the end of the sentence equals x.

  Example: The length of a rectangle <u>is</u> 4 more than the <u>width</u>.

  Since "width" is at the end of the sentence, Width = x.

- Read backwards from the end of the sentence to get the other dimension (here, length).

- The other dimension is one of these: x + some number, x – some number, $2x$, $2x$ + some number, $2x$ – some number, $3x$, $3x$ + some number, $3x$ – some number, etc.

- Translations:

two times, twice	$2x$
three times, thrice	$3x$
more than, increased by	+ the number
less than, fewer, decreased by	– the number
is	=

  The <u>length</u> of a rectangle <u>is four more than the width</u>.

- Reading backwards from the last word, the statement doesn't say "twice the width" or "three times the width," etc., which would mean $2x$ and $3x$. It doesn't say "ten times the width," which would mean $10x$. It just says "the width," which means x (from above).

- It says "more than," which means "+ the number."

- The number, found right before "more than," is 4.

- Reading backwards further, it says "is" and then "the length."

- Altogether, reading the statement backwards: "The width + the number 4 is the length."

  $$\text{So } x + 4 = \text{Length}$$

  Example: The <u>length</u> of a rectangle is <u>2 more than three times</u> the <u>width</u>.

- The word after "is," at or near the end of the sentence, is width. Width = x.

- Reading backwards, it does say "three times the width," which means $3x$.

- The statement says "more than," which means "+ the number."

- And the number, found right before "more than," is 2.

(continued)

- Reading backwards further, it says "is" and then "the length."

- Altogether, reading the statement backwards: "Three times the width + the number 2 is the length.

$$\text{So } 3x + 2 = \text{Length}$$

Step 2. Use a formula to find the area or perimeter asked for in the second sentence.

The area formula: (Area Number) = (Length) × (Width)

Multiply out, then move all terms to one side and solve as you would a quadratic equation.

The perimeter formula: (Perimeter Number) = (Length) + (Length) + (Width) + (Width)

Add out and solve for x.

Example: Find the length and width if the perimeter is 16. (Using Width = x and Length = $x + 4$)

$$(16) = (x + 4) + (x + 4) + (x) + (x) \qquad 16 = 4x + 8 \qquad 8 = 4x \qquad x = 2$$

So Width is 2 and Length is (2) + 4, or 6.

Problems, 23. Word Problems with Shapes and Dimensions

Rewrite in mathematical form:

1. The length of a rectangle is 6 more than the width.

2. The perimeter of a rectangle is twice the length plus twice the width.

3. The height of a triangle is 5 more than the base.

4. The length of a rectangle is the width increased by 2.

5. The length of a square is equal to the width times itself divided by itself.

24. Word Problems: Coin Problems

Coin problems ask you to find out how many nickels, dimes, or other coins a person has. To solve a coin problem, identify the **cents** values of each coin (a quarter = 25 cents). Identify the total **number of coins**. Identify **in cents** the total value of the money the person has.

Example:
Jane has nickels and dimes. She has 15 coins. Jane has a total of $1.25.

Coin #1: Nickel's value	= 5 cents
Coin #2: Dime's value	= 10 cents
Total number of coins	= 15
Total money in cents	= 125 cents
x will equal the amount of Coin #1	

(Coin #1 cent value) (x) + (Coin #2 cent value) (Total amount coins – x) = Total cents she has

(5) (x) + (10)(15 – x)	= 125 cents
$5x + 150 - 10x$	= 125
$-5x + 150$	= 125
$-5x$	= –25
x	= 5
5 nickels, (15 coins – 5)	= 10 dimes

Problems with More Than Two Different Coins

Usually there'll be equal amounts of two of the coins. For example, in a problem with dimes, nickels, and quarters, there might be the same number of nickels and dimes. There might be twice as many ($2x$) quarters or three times as many quarters ($3x$) or three times as many less 4 quarters ($3x - 4$), etc. Put this part in the formula where it says "here."

(Coin #1 value) (x) + (Coin #2 value) (x) + (Coin #3 value) (Total amount coins – (here)) = Total $ in ¢

Example:
Ed has nickels, dimes, and quarters. He has the same number of nickels and dimes, but twice as many quarters. He has 20 total coins. The coins amount to $3.25.

(continued)

Coin #1 = nickel = 5¢
Coin #2 = dime = 10¢
Coin #3 = quarter = 25¢
Total coins = 20 coins
Total cents = 325 cents
There are twice ($2x$) as many quarters as the other coins.
x will equal the amounts of Coins #1 and #2.

(5) (x) + (10) (x) + (25) (20 – ($2x$))	= 325 cents
(5) (x) + (10) (x) + (25) (20 – $2x$)	= 325 cents
$5x + 10x + 500 - 50x$	= 325
$-35x + 500$	= 325
$-35x$	= -175
x	= 5

5 nickels, 5 dimes, and twice as many (10) quarters

Important: Remember to distribute the minus sign through the "here" part of the formula (line 2 of the solving above).

Problems, 24. Word Problems: Coin Problems

Set up and solve these coin problems:

1. Mike has dimes and quarters. He has 18 coins. Mike has a total of $4.20. How many of each does he have?

2. Sondra has nickels and quarters. She has $2.00. She has 16 coins. How many of each does she have?

3. Stu has dimes and half-dollars. He has $1.90. He has seven coins. How many of each does he have?

4. Ian has nickels, dimes, and quarters. He has the same number of quarters and dimes. He has $1.65. He has 13 coins. How many of each does he have?

5. Rachel has pennies and nickels. She has $1.20. She has 36 coins. How many of each does she have?

25. Mixture Problems with Nuts and Candy

In these mixture problems, food items costing different amounts are mixed. A tip for solving these problems is to convert prices to cents ($2.25 = 225¢).

Example:

A grocer mixes <u>nuts costing 50¢/lb. (a pound)</u> and <u>raisins costing 70¢/lb.</u> to make a <u>30-pound mixture to sell for 60¢ a pound</u>. How many pounds of nuts and how many pounds of raisins did the grocer mix?

Formula when you don't know the quantities of the foods being mixed:

(¢ cost # 1)(x) + (¢ cost #2)(amount of mix − x) = (¢ cost of mix) (amount of mix)

$$(50)\,(x) + (70)\,(30 - x) = (60)\,(30)$$
$$50x + 2100 - 70x \quad = 1800$$
$$-20x + 2100 \quad\quad = 1800$$
$$-20x \quad\quad\quad\quad = -300$$
$$x \quad\quad\quad\quad\quad = 15$$

cost of #1 50¢/lb.
cost of #2 70¢/lb.
cost of mix 60¢/lb.
amount of #1 unknown
amount of #2 unknown
amount of mix 30 lbs.

15 pounds of (#1) nuts, (30 total − 15) = 15 pounds of raisins

Formula when you know the first quantity, but not the second:

(¢ cost #1) (amount #1) + (¢ cost #2) (x) = (¢ cost of mix) (amount #1 + x)

Example:

A grocer takes <u>10 pounds of nuts costing 70¢/lb.</u> and mixes them with <u>raisins costing 50¢/lb.</u> to make a <u>mix costing 60¢/lb.</u> How many pounds of the raisins should the grocer use, and what was the total cost of the raisins?

$$70\,(10) + (50)\,(x) \quad = (60)\,(10 + x)$$
$$700 + 50x \quad\quad\quad = 600 + 60x$$
$$700 - 600 \quad\quad\quad = 60x - 50x$$
$$100 \quad\quad\quad\quad\quad = 10x$$
$$x \quad\quad\quad\quad\quad\quad = 10$$

cost of #1 70¢/lb.
cost of #2 50¢/lb.
cost of mix 60¢/lb.
amount of #1 10 lbs.
amount of #2 unknown
amount of mix unknown

The unknown (x value) was the quantity of raisins. x is 10 pounds of #2 (raisins), plus 10 pounds of nuts, makes 20 pounds total.

Formula when you don't know the price of the mixture:

(¢ cost # 1) (amount #1) + (¢ cost #2) (amount #2) = (x) (amount of mixture)

Example:

A grocer mixes <u>10 pounds of nuts costing 60¢/lb.</u> with <u>30 pounds of raisins costing 80¢/ lb.</u> to make <u>40 pounds of a mixture costing how much?</u>

(continued)

$$
\begin{array}{ll}
(60)\ (10) + (80)\ (30) & = x\ (40) \\
600 + 2400 & = 40x \\
3000 & = 40x \\
75 & = x
\end{array}
$$

cost of #1 60¢/lb.
cost of #2 80¢/lb.
cost of mix unknown
amount of #1 10 lbs.
amount of #2 30 lbs.
amount of mix 40 lbs.

The unknown (x value) was the price (in cents) of the mix—75 cents a pound.

Problems, 25. *Mixture Problems with Nuts and Candy*

Set up and solve these mixture problems:

1. A grocer has peanuts selling for $1.50/lb. and raisins selling for $1.25/lb. He mixed how many pounds of each to make a mixture of 10 pounds at $1.30/lb.?

2. A grocer has walnuts selling for $4.00/lb. and dried mango pieces selling for $2.75/lb. How many pounds of each will make a 10-pound mixture costing $3.25/lb.?

3. Alex has dried apricots he sells for $.80/lb. and dried apples he sells for $1.20/lb. How many pounds of each will go into making a 20-pound mixture that he sells for $.84/lb.?

4. Pete has honey-roasted peanuts and plain peanuts he sells for $.70/lb. and $.50/lb., respectively. How many pounds of each will go into making a mix of 10 pounds costing $.54/lb.?

5. Pele has peanuts he sells for $.40/lb. and candy he sells for $1.00/lb. How many pounds of each will go into making a mix of 10 pounds he sells for $.52/lb.?

26. Chemical Mixture Word Problems

In chemical mixture problems, you find the amount or percentage of a chemical in a mixture. Follow these tips:

- You mix two quantities of chemicals to get a mixture quantity.

- You do not necessarily have to concern yourself with what the chemicals are.

- Chemicals are measured in grams, liters, or deciliters; these are just amounts.

- Each quantity has a "percentage of solution concentration," such as 10%.

- "Percents" are written like "cents" you find on a store receipt. .20 is 20 cents on a receipt; it is also 20%. But .5 on a receipt is .50 . . . 50 cents.

Formula when you don't know a mixture's percentage:
(Amount of first thing) (% of first thing) + (second amount) (% of second thing) = (total amount) (% of mix)

> *Example:*
> You combine <u>10 grams of 30%</u> iodine solution with <u>20 grams of 40%</u> iodine solution. What is the <u>percentage</u> of iodine <u>in the mixture</u>?

$$(10)(.30) + (20)(.40) \qquad = (30)(x)$$
$$3 + 8 \qquad\qquad\qquad = 30x$$
$$11 \qquad\qquad\qquad\qquad = 30x$$
$$x \qquad\qquad\qquad\qquad = 11/30 \text{ or } .366 \approx 37 \text{ (per)cents}$$
$$\qquad\qquad\qquad\qquad\qquad \text{on a receipt.}$$

Quantity #1 = 10 grams, 30%
Quantity #2 = 20 grams, 40%
Mix = 10 + 20 (=30), unknown %

> The percentage of iodine in the mixture is approximately 37%.

Formula when you don't know the quantities being mixed:
(% of first thing) (x) + (% of second thing) (total grams − x) = (% of third thing) (total grams)

> *Example:*
> You mix a <u>20%</u> iodine solution with a <u>30%</u> iodine solution and you make <u>20</u> grams of a <u>25%</u> iodine mixture. How many grams were each of the two solutions that you mixed?

$$(.20)(x) + (.30)(20 - x) \qquad = (.25)(20)$$
$$.20x + 6 - .30x \qquad\qquad = 5$$
$$-.1x \qquad\qquad\qquad\qquad = -1$$
$$x \qquad\qquad\qquad\qquad\quad = -1 \div -.1$$
$$x \qquad\qquad\qquad\qquad\quad = 10$$

Quantity #1 = 20%, unknown
Quantity #2 = 30%, unknown
Mix = 20 grams

> The unknown (x-value) is for the first chemical solution, so there are 10 grams of it. (20 total − 10) = 10 grams for the second solution.

(continued)

When you have pure water in a problem:
Pure water has 0% of anything chemical in it. Pure water = 0 percentage.

You mix <u>10 grams</u> of an iodine solution with <u>30 grams pure water</u> to make a mixture of <u>40 grams of 20% iodine solution</u>. What is the percentage of iodine in the first solution?

$(10)(x) + (30)(0) = (40)(.20)$

$10x + 0 \qquad = 8$

$10x \qquad\quad = 8$

$x \qquad\qquad = .80$

Quantity #1 = 10 grams, unknown
Quantity #2 = 30 grams, 0%
Mix = 40 grams, 20%

Solution #1 (the unknown) is 80% iodine.

Problems, 26. Chemical Mixture Word Problems

1. You mix an unknown amount of a 50% acid solution with a second solution that is 25% acid. How much of each should you mix to obtain 10 liters of a 40% acid solution?

2. How much of a 70% alcohol solution should be mixed with water (a 0% alcohol solution) to obtain 21 liters of a 30% alcohol solution?

3. How much of a 10% acid solution should be mixed with a 5% acid solution to obtain 20 liters of an 8% acid solution?

4. How many gallons of a 15% acid solution should be mixed with how many gallons of a 20% acid solution to obtain 30 gallons of an 18% acid solution?

5. How many ml of a 20% hydrochloric acid solution and how many ml of a 60% hydrochloric acid solution should be used to obtain 60 ml of a 50% hydrochloric acid solution?

6. How many ml of a 20% alcohol solution must be mixed with how many ml of a 50% solution to obtain 24 ml of a 30% solution?

7. How many ml of a 30% sulfuric acid solution and how many ml of a 70% sulfuric acid solution should be mixed to obtain 100 ml of a 40% solution?

27. "Can do a job in . . ." Word Problems

Here are tips for doing three types of work word problems.

When two people or companies team together to do a job:
Identify how long it takes the first person to do the whole job alone. Identify the time it takes the second person to do the whole job alone. Use the formula:

$$\frac{1}{\text{Time for \#1 alone}} + \frac{1}{\text{Time for \#2 alone}} = \frac{1}{x}$$

Example:

If Bill can weed the garden in 10 hours and Rhoda can weed the garden in 12 hours, how long will it take them to weed the garden, if they work together?

$$\frac{1}{10} + \frac{1}{12} = \frac{1}{x}$$

$$^6(60x)\frac{1}{10} + {}^5(60x)\frac{1}{12} = (60x)\frac{1}{x}$$

> Bill alone = 10 hours
> Rhoda alone = 12 hours
> Common multiple = 60 x or add fractions the new way (see page 5).

$$6x + 5x = 60$$

$$11x = 60$$

$$x = \frac{60}{11} \text{ hours or } 5\frac{5}{11} \text{ hours, working together.}$$

OR 5 hours and $27\frac{1}{2}$ minutes (from $\frac{5}{11}$ times 60 minutes).

When more than two people or companies work together:
Continue making fractions on the left side of the equation.

$$\frac{1}{\text{Time for \#1 alone}} + \frac{1}{\text{Time for \#2 alone}} + \frac{1}{\text{Time for \#3 alone}} = \frac{1}{x}$$

When a person does a job in a "fraction" time:
If Bill can do a job in two and two-thirds hours, and Fred can do a job in four hours, working together, how long will it take them?

$$\frac{1}{8/3} + \frac{1}{4} = \frac{1}{x}$$

$$\frac{1 \text{ times } {}^3/_8}{} + \frac{1}{4} = \frac{1}{x}$$

$$\underset{16x}{2} \qquad \underset{16x}{4} \quad 16x$$

> As a fraction, $2^2/_3$ is $^8/_3$. One divided by $^8/_3$ is the same as 1 times the reciprocal of $^8/_3$. $1 \times {}^3/_8 = {}^3/_8$.

$$\frac{3}{8} + \frac{1}{4} = \frac{1}{x}$$

> Common denominator is $16x$ or you can add fractions the new way (see page 5).

$$6x + 4x = 16$$

$$10x = 16 \quad x = {}^{16}/_{10} \text{ or 1.6 hours (or 1 hour 36 minute)}$$

 The You Can Do It! Guide to Algebra

Problems, 27. "Can do a job in . . ." Word Problems

1. Pete can weed the garden in six hours. Paul can weed the garden in five hours. Mary can weed the garden in four hours. How long will it take them to weed the garden together?

2. Mel can clean the diner in two hours. It takes Alice only one and a half hours to do the same job. Together, how long will it take them to clean the diner?

3. Randy can mow the lawn in two hours. His sister can mow it in three hours. Together, how long will it take them to do the job?

4. Mike can deliver papers in two and a half hours. Steve only needs one hour to do the same job. How long will it take if they combine their efforts to deliver the papers?

5. Ian can shovel snow in two hours. It takes Don only an hour. But together, how long will it take them?

28. Rate, Time, and Distance Problems

Here are some tips for solving word problems that ask how long it will take for vehicles traveling toward each other to meet:

- Identify how fast each is going. Identify how far apart they start out.

- Identify if they start out at the same time, or if they leave at different times.

Formula when they start out simultaneously:

(Speed #1) (x) + (Speed #2) (x) = Miles apart

Example:

Two cars, traveling at 50 and 60 mph, respectively, leave from places 220 miles apart. How long does it take for them to meet?

$$(50)(x) + (60)(x) = 220$$
$$(50)(x) + (60)(x) = 220$$
$$110x = 220$$
$$x = 2$$

| Speed #1 = 50 |
| Speed #2 = 60 |
| Miles apart = 220 |

It takes them two hours to meet.

Formula when the second car delays its departure:

(Speed of #1) (x) + (Speed of #2) (x – delay) = Miles apart

Example:

Two cars will meet from places 120 miles apart. One will go 20 mph and the other 30 mph; the car going 30 mph delays its departure an hour after car #1 leaves. How long will it take the cars to meet?

$$(20)(x) + (30)(x - 1) = 120$$
$$20x + 30x - 30 = 120$$
$$50x - 30 = 120$$
$$50x = 150$$
$$x = 3$$

| Speed #1 = 20 |
| Speed #2 = 30 |
| Miles apart = 120 |
| #2 delays 1 hour |

It takes three hours for car #1.
3 – 1-hour delay = 2. It takes two hours for car #2.

Formula when the second car departs early:

(Speed #1) (x) + (Speed #2) (x + head start) = Miles apart

Example:

Two cars, from 260 miles apart, traveling at 30 and 50 mph, respectively, will meet. The car going 50 mph departs two hours early. How long will it take the cars to meet?

(continued)

$$\begin{aligned}
(30)\,(x) + (50)\,(x + 2) &= 260 \\
30x + 50x + 100 &= 260 \\
80x + 100 &= 260 \\
80x &= 160 \\
x &= 2
\end{aligned}$$

Speed #1 = 30
Speed #2 = 50
Miles apart = 260
Head start for #2 is 2 hours.

It takes two hours for car #1.
2 + 2-hour head start = 4. It takes four hours for car #2.

- If the first car gets a head start of two hours, it's the same as the second car being delayed two hours, so you can use the "second car delay" formula.

Problems, 28. Rate, Time, and Distance Problems

1. Two cars, traveling toward each other at 50 and 60 mph, respectively, leave from points 880 miles apart. How long is it before they meet?

2. Two cars, traveling toward each other at 60 and 70 mph, respectively leave from points 260 miles apart. How long will it be before they meet?

3. One car going 50 mph leaves three hours before a second car going 40 mph leaves. If they meet in 420 miles, how many hours did it take for the cars to meet?

4. Two cars, 400 miles apart, decide to travel 50 mph until they meet. However, one car leaves two hours earlier than the first. How long after the first car left will they meet?

5. Two cars, 700 miles apart, decide to travel to meet. One leaves four hours ahead and travels at 30 mph. Then the second leaves going 50 mph. How long before they meet?

29. Rate, Time, and Distance Problems: Alternating Speeds

In one type of word problem, a vehicle will travel at different speeds to reach a destination. You are asked to find out how many hours the vehicle traveled at each speed.

Formula when a vehicle changes speeds en route to its destination:

(Speed #1) (x) + (Speed #2) (Total time − x) = Total distance traveled

Example:
A car travels 20 mph and 50 mph on a trip of 580 miles. The trip lasts 14 hours. How much time did the car travel 20 mph and how much time did it travel 50 mph?

$$(20)\,(x) + (50)\,(14 - x) = 580$$
$$20x + 700 - 50x \quad\quad = 580$$
$$-30x + 700 \quad\quad = 580$$
$$-30x \quad\quad = -120$$
$$x \quad\quad = 4$$

Speed #1 = 20 mph
Speed #2 = 50 mph
Total time = 14 hours
Total miles = 580

The car traveled four hours at 20 mph.
It traveled 10 hours at 50 mph (14 total − 4).

Problems, 29. Rate, Time, and Distance Problems: Alternating Speeds

1. A car goes 60 mph and 30 mph, alternating between the speeds. If the car travels 750 miles total over 17 hours total, for how many hours did it go at each speed?

2. A boat travels 30 mph and 20 mph, alternating. The boat goes 240 miles in 10 hours. How many hours did it travel at each speed?

3. A car goes 25 mph and 50 mph, alternating between the speeds. If it goes 650 miles in 15 hours, how many hours did it go at each speed?

30. Rate, Time, and Distance Problems: Water or Air Currents

Some rate, time, and distance problems have a boat and a river, or a plane and an air current. For example, a boat goes its speed (say, 10 mph) and the current of the river flows its own speed (say, 5 mph downstream).

The river current propels the boat along when the boat is going downstream. The current hinders the boat when the boat goes upstream. The situations are similar to running with the wind at one's back versus running into a gust of wind. The wind helps you along, or holds you back.

Formula when the current and the vehicle's speeds are unknown:

Example:
A boat takes three hours to go downstream 30 miles. Then it returns upstream the 30 miles, taking five hours. If the boat's rate was constant (kept the same), what is (a) the boat's rate and (b) the rate of the river current?

The unknowns are speeds (rates). Call the rate of the boat r and the rate of the current c.

> Distance downstream: 30 miles
> Distance upstream: 30 miles
> Time downstream: 3 hours
> Time upstream: 5 hours
> Rate of boat: r
> Rate of current: c

Step 1. (Time downstream) $(r + c)$ + (Time upstream) $(r - c)$ = Total traveled

$$(3)\,(r + c) + 5\,(r - c) = 60$$
$$3r + 3c + 5r - 5c = 60$$
$$8r - 2c = 60 \quad \text{(Step 1 answer)}$$

> $8\,(r) - 2\,(c) = 60$
> $8\,(10 - 1c) - 2c = 60$
> $80 - 8c - 2c = 60$
> $-8c - 2c = -20$
> $-10c = -20$
> $c = 2$ (current = 2)
> Return to Step 2
> answer.
> $r = 10 - 1\,(c)$
> $r = 10 - 1\,(2)$
> $r = 10 - 2$
> $r = 8$ (rate of boat = 8)

Step 2. (Time downstream) $(r + c)$ = Distance downstream

$$3\,(r + c) = 30$$
$$3r + 3c = 30$$

Solve for either variable.

$$3r = 30 - 3c$$
$$r = 30/3 - 3c/3$$
$$r = 10 - 1c \quad \text{(Step 2 answer)}$$

Step 3. Return to the Step 1 answer. Put parentheses around the variables (letters). Now it should look like: $8(r) - 2(c) = 60$.

Step 4. Plug what r equaled from the Step 2 answer $(10 - 1c)$, into the (r) parentheses of the Step 1 answer. (Erase r and write in $(10 - 1c)$. Now follow the steps in the preceding box.

Problems, 30. Rate, Time, and Distance Problems: Water or Air Currents

1. A man went 27 miles downstream in a boat taking three hours to do it; it took him three times as long (nine hours) to return upstream the 27 miles. What was the rate of the boat in still water and the rate of the current?

2. A man took three hours to go 24 miles downstream, and six hours to return the 24 miles upstream. What was the rate of the boat in still water and the rate of the current?

3. A woman took three hours to go 42 miles downstream, and six hours to return upstream all 42 miles. What was the rate of the boat in still water and the rate of the current?

4. Flying with the wind, Wonder Woman flew in her aircraft 300 miles in five hours. To return the 300 miles, she took six hours, flying against the wind. What was the rate of the superplane in still air and the rate of the air current?

5. A plane goes 2000 miles in five hours flying against the wind. The same plane takes four hours to fly the same distance with the wind. What's the rate of the plane in still air, and the rate of the air current?

Graphing and Solving for *x*

31. Plotting Points on a Graph

- The graph shown below is called the "coordinate axes."

- The horizontal (across) number line is called the *x*-axis.

- The vertical (up and down) number line is called the *y*-axis.

- There are four "quadrants" (zones), going counterclockwise, labeled I, II, III, and IV.

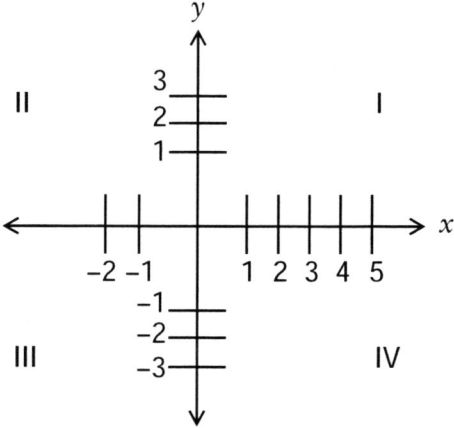

- Each place on the graph has an across value and an up-or-down value.

- The across value is called the *x*-value; the up-or-down value is the *y*-value.

- The values are put into parentheses: (*x*-value, *y*-value)

- First you go across to the *x*-value location, then you go up-down to the *y*-value location.

This is where you place (plot) a dot (point).

Example: Plot (1, 2).

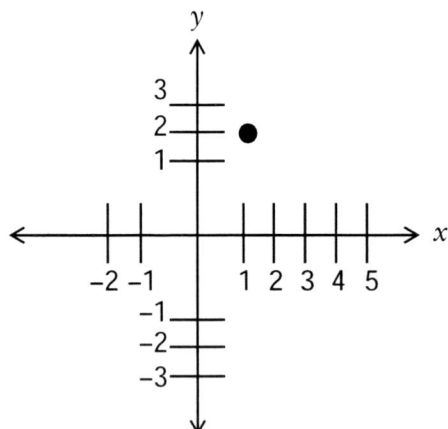

The numbers (1,2) mean one to the
 right, two up.
A positive *x* means to the right.
A negative *x* means to the left.
A positive *y* means up.
A negative *y* means down.

Example: Plot (–2, –3).

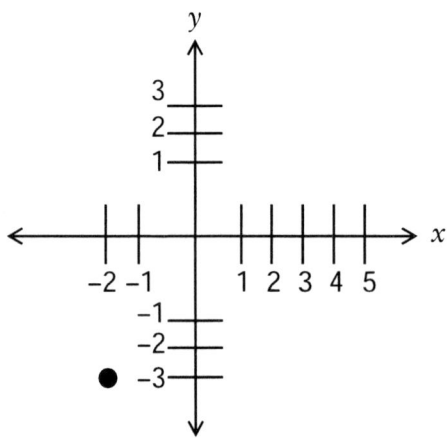

The numbers (–2,–3) mean
two to the left,
three down,
and place a dot.

The You Can Do It! Guide to Algebra

Problems, 31. Plotting Points on a Graph

Plot the following points on a graph:

1. (1, 4)

2. (–2, –5)

3. (–1, 4)

4. (0, –3)

5. (4, –1)

32. Finding Points from an Equation

Points

An example of a point (or "point pair") is (1, 5). The first number is called the *x*-coordinate or *x*-value, and the second number is called the *y*-coordinate or *y*-value. This point (1, 5) has an *x*-coordinate of 1, and a *y*-coordinate of 5, and the (*x*-value, *y*-value) are written in alphabetical order.

A table like the one here plays an important role in finding points. It has a column for *x*-values and a column for *y*-values.

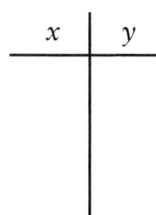

The steps below show how to find two points from the following equation:
$$y = 2x + 1$$

Step 1. Put parentheses around the variables (letters) in the equation.
$$(y) = 2 (x) + 1$$

Step 2. Pick a letter that you will replace with 0. It's good to pick the letter that looks like it's in the midst of action (operations). Here the (*x*) letter looks like it's doing more than the (*y*).

Step 3. Write 0 under that letter's column in the table.

x	*y*
0	

Step 4. Taking the equation, replace the letter you chose with 0.
$$(y) = 2 (0) + 1$$

Solve for the other letter.
$$(y) = 2 (0) + 1$$
$$y = 0 + 1$$
$$y = 1$$

Step 5. Write the value you got as an answer (from Step 4) in its column of the table.

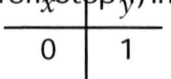

The first point you got is (0,1).

x	*y*
0	1

Step 6. Return to Step 2 but this time pick a letter you will replace with 1 or any number you like. It is simpler to work with 0 or 1, but you may choose any number. After getting two points, plot them on a graph, and draw a line through them. Also note that though two points are sufficient for a line, in class you usually have to find three points.

(continued)

         The You Can Do It! Guide to Algebra

Problems, 32. Finding Points from an Equation

Find two points on each line.

1. $y = x + 5$

2. $y = 2x + 2$

3. $y = 4x + 4$

4. $y = 5x - 6$

5. $y = 10x - 2$

6. $y = -2x$

7. $y = -3x + 3$

33. Finding the Distance Between Two Points

Step 1. Select a Point #1 and a Point #2.

For example, if you have (4, 2) and (0, 5), you could decide that Point #1 will be (4, 2) and Point #2 will be (0, 5). This is totally arbitrary.

Step 2. Write out the values from each point.

Point #1	(4, 2)	Point #2	(0, 5)
x value = 4		x value = 0	
y value = 2		y value = 5	

Step 3. Plug these values into this portion of the distance formula:

(Point #2 y-value – Point #1 y-value)^2 + (Point #2 x-value – Point #1 x-value)^2

Here, we have $(5-2)^2$ + $(0-4)^2$

$(3)^2$ + $(-4)^2$

9 + 16

25

Step 4. Take the square root of this answer.

The square root of 25 is 5.

Step 5. That's the distance between the two points.

The distance is five units.

Problems, 33. Finding the Distance Between Two Points

Find the distance between the two points.

1. (0, 0) and (4, 0)

2. (–2, 0) and (0, 0)

3. (4, 0) and (4, –4)

4. (1, 1) and (5, 2)

5. (8, 1) and (–2, 3)

34. Finding Slope, *y*-Intercept, and the Equation of a Line

Suppose you are given two points and asked to find the equation of a line. For example, you are given the points (1, 4) and (2, 5) and asked to find the equation of the line that you can draw through them.

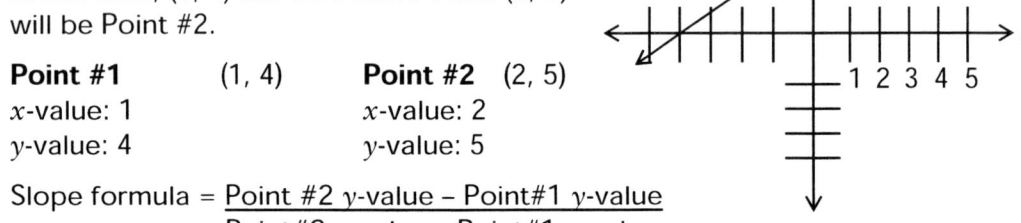

Follow these steps:

Step 1. Find the slope (called *m*)

Call one point Point #1 and the other Point #2. In this case, (1, 4) will be Point #1 and (2, 5) will be Point #2.

Point #1   (1, 4)   **Point #2**   (2, 5)
x-value: 1   *x*-value: 2
y-value: 4   *y*-value: 5

Slope formula = $\dfrac{\text{Point \#2 } y\text{-value} - \text{Point\#1 } y\text{-value}}{\text{Point\#2 } x\text{-value} - \text{Point\#1 } x\text{-value}}$

Here, *m* (the slope) = $\dfrac{5-4}{2-1} = \dfrac{1}{1} = 1$

Step 2. Choose either Point #1 or Point #2 to finish the problem with.

Point #1   (1, 4)
x-value: 1
y-value: 4

Step 3. Plug *x*-value, *y*-value, and *m* (the slope) into the slope-intercept formula
(*y*-value) = (*m*) (*x*-value) + *b*
and solve for *b*.   (*y*-value) = (*m*) (*x*-value) + *b*
$$4 = (1)(1) + b$$
$$4 = 1 + b$$
$$3 = b$$

b is the *y*-intercept, the place on the *y*-axis where the line cuts through.

Step 4. Plug only *m* and *b* into
$$y = (m)\,x + (b)$$
$$y = (1)\,x + 3$$
$$y = x + 3$$

This is the "equation of the line."

Note: Some problems start with a point and a *y*-intercept value, say *y*-intercept = 2. The *y*-intercept value, written as a point, is (0, the value here). Here, the *y*-intercept value of 2 is really the point (0, 2).

• If you are given the slope (called *m*) to start, skip Step 1.

(continued)

- If you are given the slope and the *y*-intercept, go directly to Step 4.

- If you are given the *y*-intercept and a point to start, make the *y*-intercept into a point and do Step 1; then go directly to Step 4.

Problems, 34. Finding Slope, y-Intercept, and the Equation of a Line

Find the equation of the line going through:

1. (–2, 3) and (–1, 4)

2. (0, 0) and (1, 6)

3. (0, 3) and (2, 13)

4. (1, 1) and (2, –2)

5. (1, 1) and (2, 5)

35. Graphing Horizontal and Vertical Lines: $y = 2$, $x = 4$

Horizontal Lines

The equation for a horizontal line is y = a number. To graph a line like this, find the number on the y-axis, and draw a horizontal line through it. You can remember that it is the y-axis because the equation is y = a number.

Example: $y = 3$.

Find the mark for 3 on the y-axis, and draw a horizontal line through it.

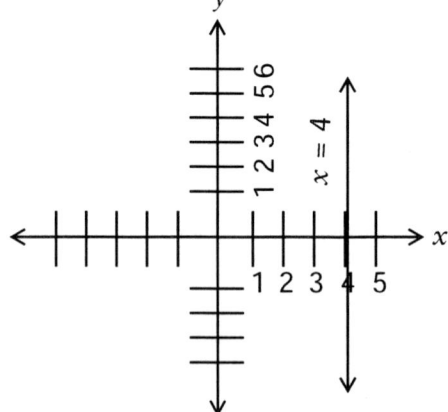

Vertical Lines

The equation for a vertical line is x = a number. To graph a vertical line, find the number's mark on the x-axis, and draw a vertical line through it. You can remember that it is the x-axis because the equation is x = a number.

Vertical lines are not functions.

Example: $x = 4$.

Problems, 35. Graphing Horizontal and Vertical Lines:
y = 2, x = 4

Graph the following horizontal and vertical lines:

1. $y = 1$

2. $x = -3$

3. $x = 0$

4. $x = 2$

5. $y = 0$

36. Graphing Inequalities

Here are some tips for graphing an inequality such as:

$$y > x + 3$$

Step 1. Replace the inequality sign (<, >, ≥, or ≤) with an equal sign.

$$y > x + 3$$
$$y = x + 3$$

Step 2. Make a table and find two points from the equation.

For $x = 0$	For $x = 1$	x	y
$(y) = (x) + 3$	$(y) = (x) + 3$	0	3
$y = (0) + 3$	$y = (1) + 3$	1	4
$y = 3$	$y = 4$		

Step 3.

- Plot the points and draw a dashed line through them if the original inequality sign was > or <. Otherwise draw a regular line.

- Select any point you know **is not** on the line, and plug its coordinate values into the **original inequality equation**.

- A good shading checkpoint is (0, 0), assuming the line doesn't go through it.

- Here, (0, 0) is OK to use. It has an x-value of 0 and a y-value of 0.

$$(y) > (x) + 3$$
$$(0) > (0) + 3$$
$$0 > 3$$

But 0 is actually not "greater than" 3 as it says. This answer is "false."

- Shade one side of the "inequality" line as shown in the diagram.

- If you get "true," shade from the line toward the shading checkpoint.

- If you get "false," shade from the line in the direction away from shading checkpoint.

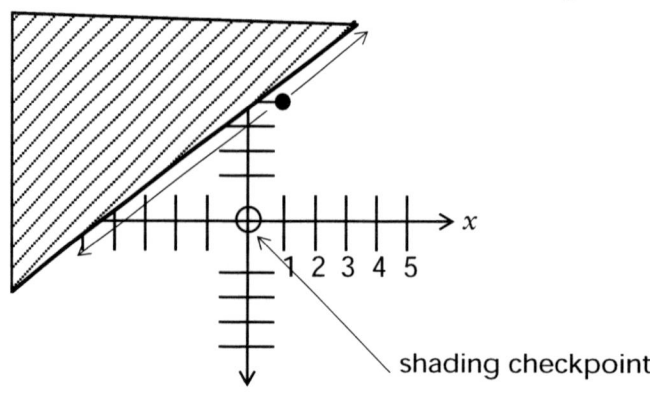

shading checkpoint

Problems, 36. Graphing Inequalities

Graph these inequalities:

1. $y > 2x$

2. $y > -3x + 1$

3. $y < 3x - 2$

4. $y > x - 4$

5. $y < 2x - 3$

37. Solving for *x*: Completing the Square

The HP–MIA–SQURT–NO ( )–SOLVE method finds *x* when you have equations that look like this:

$$x^2 + 4x - 1 = 0$$

Step 1. Move all the numbers (here, –1) to the right side of the equation.

$$x^2 + 4x - 1 = 0$$
$$x^2 + 4x \quad = 1$$

Step 2. $\quad\quad\quad\quad x^2 + 4x = 1$

HP Take **H**alf of the *x*-term's coefficient, including its sign, and put it in a **P**arentheses with *x* to the left of it. Raise the parentheses to the second power.

$$(x + 2)^2 = 1$$

To get half, you can always multiply by 1/2. The *x* term's coefficient is +4. 4/1 times 1/2 = 4/2 = +2.

Step 3. Take the number that went into the parentheses (here, +2) and **M**ultiply it by **I**tself.

MIA **A**dd this number to the right side of the equation.

$$+2 \times +2 = 4$$
$$(x + 2)^2 = 1 + 4$$
$$(x + 2)^2 = 5$$

Step 4. Take away the exponent from the parentheses, and place a **SQU**are **R**oo**T** over the right side of the equation, putting a ± "plus or minus" sign in front of it.

SQURT $\quad\quad\quad (x + 2) = \pm \sqrt{5}$

Step 5. Remove the parentheses.

NO ( ) $\quad\quad\quad x + 2 = \pm \sqrt{5}$

Step 6. Move the +2 to the other side of the equation as a –2.

SOLVE $\quad\quad\quad x = -2 \pm \sqrt{5}$

To remember this method, think up a memory device that works for you. For example: A one-time presidential candidate who worked in computers (HP), tried to bring home the MIA's, is a (SQURT), doesn't believe in hiding things (NO ( )), and wants to SOLVE the nation's problems.

Review: Move the –1 to the right side of the equation, take half of +4 which is +2, and put it into $(x + 2)$. Multiply 2×2 and add it to the right side. Then take away the 2 exponent, and take the ± square root of the right side of the equation.

(continued)

Remove the ( ). Move the +2 to the right side as a –2, putting this to the left of the ± square root.

Problems, 37. Solving for x: Completing the Square

Complete the square:

1. $x^2 + 4x + 2 = 0$

2. $x^2 + 6x + 2 = 0$

3. $x^2 + 2x + 5 = 0$

4. $x^2 - 2x - 4 = 0$

5. $x^2 - 8x + 1 = 0$

38. Solving for *x*: The Quadratic Formula

The quadratic formula finds *x* when you have (quadratic) equations like these:

$$2x^2 + 6x - 1 = 0 \qquad 6x - 2 = 0 \qquad x^2 - 2 = 0$$

Step 1. Move all terms to one side of the equation, so the other side equals 0.

Example:
$$x^2 + 6x \quad = 1$$
$$x^2 + 6x - 1 = 0$$

Step 2. Identify the coefficients. First put 1's before any variable that doesn't have a number before it.

$$x^2 + 6x - 1 = 0$$
$$1x^2 + 6x - 1 = 0$$

a = The coefficient (the sign and the number that comes before) of x^2.

b = The coefficient (the sign and the number that comes before) of *x*.

c = The number.

$$a = 1 \qquad b = 6 \qquad c = -1$$

Step 3. Plug *a*, *b*, and *c* into the "quadratic formula."

$$x = \frac{-(b) \pm \sqrt{(b)^2 - 4(a)(c)}}{2(a)}$$

$$x = \frac{-(6) \pm \sqrt{(6)^2 - 4(1)(-1)}}{2(-1)}$$

$$x = \frac{-(6) \pm \sqrt{36 - (-4)}}{-2}$$

$$x = \frac{-6 \pm \sqrt{36 + 4}}{-2}$$

$$x = \frac{-6 \pm \sqrt{40}}{-2}$$

$$x = \frac{-6 \pm \sqrt{(2 \times 2) \times (2 \times 2) \times 5}}{-2}$$

$$x = \frac{-6 \pm (2 \times 2)\sqrt{5}}{-2}$$

$$x = \frac{-6 \pm 4\sqrt{5}}{-2}$$

$$x = \frac{-6 + 4\sqrt{5}}{-2} \text{ and } \frac{-6 - 4\sqrt{5}}{-2}$$

There are two answers. The first takes the + of the ± and the second takes the −.

Problems, 38. Solving for x*: The Quadratic Formula*

Solve for x using the quadratic formula:

1. $x^2 + 4x + 4 = 0$

2. $x^2 + 6x + 9 = 0$

3. $x^2 + 2x + 1 = 0$

4. $x^2 - 2x - 1 = 0$

5. $x^2 - 8x + 16 = 0$

6. $x^2 - 4x + 3 = 0$

39. Solving for *x* with Fractions: Cross-Multiply and Divide

Cross-multiply and divide to find *x* in equations that look like this:

$$\frac{2}{3} = \frac{x}{6}$$

Step 1. Cross-multiply diagonally upwards.

$$6 \times 2 = 12 \qquad\qquad 3 \times x = 3x$$

$$\frac{2}{3} \diagup\!\!\!\!\!\diagdown \frac{x}{6}$$

Step 2. Set the products equal.

$$12 = 3x$$

Step 3. Divide through by the coefficient of *x*.

$$\frac{12}{3} = \frac{\cancel{3}x}{\cancel{3}}$$

$$4 = x$$

Follow these steps to solve for *x* when the equation contains an expression, such as *x* + 2:

Example: $\qquad \dfrac{10}{3} = \dfrac{x+2}{6}$

Step 1. Before you start cross-multiplication, put parentheses around the *x* + 2 as it is an "expression" (it has a + or − in it). Expressions are treated as a unit.

$$6 \times 10 = 60 \qquad\qquad 3\,(x+2) = 3x + 6$$

$$\frac{10}{3} \diagup\!\!\!\!\!\diagdown \frac{(x+2)}{6}$$

Step 2. Isolate the variable.

$$
\begin{aligned}
60 &= 3x + 6 \\
60 - 6 &= 3x \\
54 &= 3x
\end{aligned}
$$

Step 3. Divide both sides by 3.

$$
\begin{aligned}
\frac{54}{3} &= \frac{\cancel{3}x}{\cancel{3}} \\[2mm]
18 &= x
\end{aligned}
$$

Problems, 39. Solving for x *with Fractions: Cross-Multiply and Divide*

Cross-multiply and divide to solve for x:

1. $\dfrac{1}{3} = \dfrac{x}{9}$

2. $\dfrac{5}{6} = \dfrac{(x+1)}{12}$

3. $\dfrac{(x+2)}{6} = \dfrac{1}{3}$

4. $\dfrac{1}{10} = \dfrac{5}{(x+5)}$

5. $\dfrac{3}{4} = \dfrac{6}{(x+2)}$

 The You Can Do It! Guide to Algebra

40. Solving for *x*: Equations with Fractions

Prerequisites: Solving Gigantic Fractions, page 90, Quadratic Formula, page 82, Completing the Square, page 80. To solve equations with fractions, fraction-subtract the new way (page 5). Or use the gigantic fractions method (page 90); start by changing whole numbers to fractions.

$$\frac{12}{x-3} - \frac{12}{x+4} = 1$$

Step 1.

$$\frac{12}{x-3} \quad \frac{12}{x+4} = 1$$

Step 2.

$$12\,(x+4) - 12\,(x-3)$$
$$12x + 48 - 12x + 36$$
$$84$$

Step 3. Multiply denominators from the crisscross.

$$(x-3)\,(x+4)$$

Step 4. Set up the fraction answer.

$$\frac{84}{(x-3)(x+4)} = 1$$

Step 5. Cross-multiply and set the products equal.

$$\frac{84}{(x-3)(x+4)} = \frac{1}{1}$$

$$84 \quad = (x-3)\,(x+4)$$
$$84 \quad = x^2 + 4x - 3x - 12$$
$$84 \quad = x^2 + 1x - 12$$

- Set to 0.
$$0 \quad = x^2 + 1x - 12 - 84$$
$$0 \quad = x^2 + 1x - 96$$

- Solve for *x* through the quadratic formula (page 82), completing the square (page 80), or factoring.

Example:

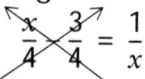

Crisscross subtract:	$\dfrac{4x-12}{16} = \dfrac{1}{x}$
Denominator product:	

Cross multiply: $4x^2 - 12x = 16$
Set to zero: $4x^2 - 12x - 16 = 0$

Solve via quadratic formula, completing the square, or factoring.

Factoring:
$$4\,(x^2 - 3x - 4) = 0$$
$$4\,(x-4)\,(x+1) = 0$$
$$x = 4 \text{ and } -1$$

The You Can Do It! Guide to Algebra

Problems, 40. Solving for x: *Equations with Fractions*

Solve these equations with fractions:

1. $\dfrac{x}{2} + \dfrac{x}{3} = 5$

2. $\dfrac{x}{5} - \dfrac{x}{7} = 2$

3. $\dfrac{7}{x-2} = \dfrac{5}{x}$

4. $\dfrac{2}{x} = \dfrac{14}{x+3}$

5. $\dfrac{3}{2x+7} = \dfrac{2}{x}$

41. Solving for *x*: Factoring Out

When there is an x^2, factor out to solve for x.

Step 1. Move every term to one side, so the other side equals 0.

Example:
$$x^2 = -9x - 20$$
$$x^2 + 9x = -20$$
$$x^2 + 9x + 20 = 0$$

Step 2. Factor the left side of the equation via "three-term" factoring.
$$x^2 + 9x + 20 = 0 \qquad 20 = 4 \times 5; \ 4 + 5 = 9.$$
$$(x + 4)(x + 5) = 0$$

Step 3. Take each parentheses separately, set it equal to 0, and solve.

$(x + 4) = 0$ $(x + 5) = 0$
$x + 4 = 0$ $x + 5 = 0$
$x = -4$ $x = -5$

Step 4. Express the solutions.

$x = -4$
$x = -5$

Example: $x^2 + 5x = 0$

Step 1. Every term is already on one side of the equation.

Step 2. Since there are not enough terms to do two-parentheses factoring, use common factoring.
$$x^2 + 5x = 0$$
$$x(x + 5) = 0$$

Step 3. Take the factor and the parentheses, and separately set to 0 and solve.

$x = 0$ $(x + 5) = 0$
         $x + 5 = 0$
         $x = -5$

Step 4. Express the solutions.

$x = -5$
$x = 0.$

Problems, 41. Solving for x: *Factoring Out*

Factor and solve.

1. $x^2 + 4x + 3 = 0$

2. $x^2 - 5x + 6 = 0$

3. $x^2 + 7x = 0$

4. $x^3 + x^2 = 0$

5. $x^2 = 7x - 12$

42. Solving Gigantic Fractions

Prerequisite: Solving for x: Equations with Fractions (page 86).

A gigantic-fraction problem has many fractions in one fraction:

$$\frac{\dfrac{x^2}{y}+\dfrac{y}{x}}{\dfrac{2}{x}-\dfrac{4x}{y^2}}$$

Step 1. Find a common denominator for **all** the fractions. The common denominator for all four fractions here is xy^2.

Step 2. Write the common denominator near each numerator of every fraction.

$$xy^2 \quad \frac{\dfrac{x^2}{y}+\dfrac{y}{x}}{\dfrac{2}{x}-\dfrac{4x}{y^2}} \quad xy^2$$
$$xy^2 \qquad\qquad\qquad xy^2$$

Step 3. Cancel the denominators with the common denominators.

$$\frac{\dfrac{x^2}{y}+\dfrac{y}{x}}{\dfrac{2}{x}-\dfrac{4x}{y^2}}$$

Step 4. All denominators should have canceled completely out.

Step 5. Multiply whatever is left of the common denominators times the numerators.

$$\frac{x^2y^1+y^3}{2y^2-4x^2}$$

Multiply only with the **neighboring** common denominators.

- The result is the final answer, unless you can factor things out from the top or bottom, and cancel. The answer above can be factored, but there is no canceling.

$$\frac{y^1(x^3-y^2)}{2y-4x}$$

The You Can Do It! Guide to Algebra

(continued)

Problems, 42. Solving Gigantic Fractions

1. $\dfrac{\dfrac{1}{x^3} + \dfrac{y}{x^2}}{\dfrac{y^2}{x^2} + \dfrac{y^3}{x^3}}$

2. $\dfrac{\dfrac{1}{a^3 b} - \dfrac{2}{a^2 b}}{\dfrac{3}{ab^2} + \dfrac{4}{a^2 b}}$

3. $\dfrac{\dfrac{4}{a^2} + \dfrac{1}{ab^2}}{\dfrac{b}{a} + \dfrac{1}{ab}}$

4. $\dfrac{\dfrac{y}{x^2} + \dfrac{2}{x}}{\dfrac{1}{x^2} - \dfrac{a}{x}}$

5. $\dfrac{\dfrac{c}{b} + \dfrac{1}{b^2}}{\dfrac{2}{b^3} + \dfrac{c^3}{b}}$

       The You Can Do It! Guide to Algebra

43. Solving Two Equations: The Substitution Method

$$x + y = 2$$
$$x - y = 0$$

- There are two equations. If the only exponents are powers of 1, they're lines.

- Lines and other equations can be graphed.

- Find where the lines (or line and circle, etc.) cross (intersect).

The Substitution Method:

- Take one equation and solve for a variable. Underline what it equals.

- In the other equation, find the same variable you solved for; put a ( ) around it.

$$x + y = 2 \text{ -----> Solving for } y \text{ ----> } y = \underline{2 - x}$$
$$x - y = 0 \text{ -----> Put ( ) around } y \text{ ----> } x - (y) = 0$$

- Take this ( ) letter variable out and put in its equivalent that you underlined.

$$y = \underline{2 - x}$$
$$x - (y) = 0 \text{ ----> } \boxed{x - (2 - x) = 0}$$

Continue and solve:
$x - (2 - x) = 0$
$x - 2 + x = 0$ Remember to distribute the − sign.
$2x - 2 = 0$
$2x = 2$ $\boxed{x = 1}$

Now return to any equation with both variables in it above, and plug in 1 for x.

$$x + y = 2$$
$$(1) + y = 2$$
$$y = 2 - 1$$
$$\boxed{y = 1}$$ The lines cross at (1, 1).

- The graphs of lines may not cross at all (if they are parallel lines). In this case, you will get a "contradiction answer" in solving, like 1 = 2. Stop and write "parallel lines, no solution."

Example:
$$y = -1x + 4$$
$$x + y = 1$$

$$y = \underline{-1x + 4}$$
$$x + (y) = 1 \text{ -------> } x + (-1x + 4) = 1$$
$$x - 1x + 4 = 1$$

4 = 1. Parallel lines, no solution.   *(continued)*

- The graphs of lines may cross in every point (if they are the same line). In this case, you will get an "identity answer" in solving, like 1 = 1. Stop and write "Infinite solutions."

Example:
$$y = -x + 1$$
$$2x + 2y = 2$$

$y = \underline{-x + 1}$

$2x + 2(y) = 2$ -----> $2x + 2(-x + 1) = 2$ $2x - 2x + 2 = 2$
$2 = 2$ Infinite solutions.

Problems, 43. Solving Two Equations: The Substitution Method

Solve by using the substitution method.

1. $2y = x + 2$
   $y = -2x + 6$

2. $3y = 15$
   $3x - 15y = 0$

3. $x + 2 = 0$
   $x + y = 5$

4. $y = 2x + 3$
   $x + y = 6$

5. $y + 3 = x$
   $3x + 4y = 16$

The You Can Do It! Guide to Algebra

44. Solving Two Equations: Addition/ Elimination Method

The addition/elimination method is a good way to solve two equations such as the following:

$$x + y = 2$$
$$x - y = 0$$

- Equations can be graphed (they may be equations of lines or circles, etc.).

- The problem is: "At what (x, y) point do the graphs (e.g., lines) cross?"

Step 1. Move the terms around if necessary to line up the equations as in the example above—x's are on the far left, then the y's, then =, then the numbers.

Step 2. Insert coefficients of 1 before variables that don't have coefficients.

$x + y = 2$
is the same as
$1x + 1y = 2$

$1x + 1y = 2$
$1x - 1y = 0$

$x - y = 0$
is the same as
$1x - 1y = 2$

- Important questions: What is the opposite of 1? Answer: –1. What is the opposite of $1x$? Answer: $-1x$. What do you get when you add opposites? Answer: 0.

- You want to "make opposites" (through multiplying) out of the x's or the y's

$10x$ $2x$	• To make opposites, you'd multiply the $2x$ by –5, to make $-10x$.	$10x$ ----> $10x$ $2x$ (–5) ----> $-10x$
$-4x$ $8x$	• To make opposites, you'd multiply the $-4x$ by 2, to make $-8x$.	$-4x$ (2) ----> $-8x$ $8x$ ----> $8x$
$2y$ $5y$	• To make opposites, you could multiply the $2y$ by 5, and the $5y$ by –2, making opposites of $10y$ and $-10y$.	$2y$ (–5) ----> $-10y$ $5y$ (–2) ----> $10y$

(continued)

Step 3. When you multiply something (in making opposites), you actually multiply the **whole row**, separately, by the same number.

$1x + 1y = 5$ • To make opposites, you $-2(1x) + -2(1y) = -2(5)$
$2x - 3y = -5$ could multiply the $1x$ row $2x - 3y = -5$
                          by -2 to get opposites of
                          $-2x$ and $2x$.

Step 4. After getting opposites (here, $-2x$ and $2x$), add the rows downward.

$$-2x - 2y = -10$$
$$\underline{2x - 3y = -5}$$
$$0 - 5y = -15$$

Step 5. Solve for the variable.

$$-5y = -15$$
$$y = 3$$

Step 6. Plug this value into the first equation, and solve for the other variable.

$$-2x - 2(3) = -10$$
$$-2x - 6 = -10$$
$$-2x = -4$$
$$x = 2$$

Step 7. State your solution. Your solution here is $x = 2$, $y = 3$, or the point $(2, 3)$.

Problems, 44. Solving Two Equations: Addition/Elimination Method

Solve by using the elimination method:

1. $x + y = 2$
   $x - y = 0$

2. $x + 3y = 5$
   $5x - 3y = 7$

3. $2x + 2y = 0$
   $4x - 2y = 12$

4. $9x - 8y = 12$
   $9x - 4y = 24$

5. $5x - 2y = -13$
   $2x + y = 11$

45. Is the Equation a Function?

Shortcuts to Stating That an Equation is Not a Function

An equation is not a function if it contains a y-variable raised to an even power, such as y^2 or y^4. Also, vertical lines are not functions because they have the equation x = some number. **Everything** is a relation.

Every x-Value is Paired with a Different y-Value

Think of x as the husband and y as the wife. Memory device: no husband (x) can have two wives (y). So no x-value can be paired with more than one y-value, or it's not a function. The points (1, 12) and (1, 8) wouldn't make a function because the x-value of 1 has two y-values of 12 **and** 8.

x	y
1	12
1	8

Not a function for the same reason.

x y

$1 \longrightarrow \begin{array}{c} 12 \\ 8 \end{array}$ Still not a function.

Anytime the same x is paired a second time with a different y, it's not a function.

Vertical Line Test

You can test whether a graph is a function by performing the "vertical line test." If a vertical line can be drawn through **two places** anywhere on the graph of a line, parabola, circle, ellipse, etc., then the graph is not a function.

This is a function. Each vertical line does not pass through two or more places on the graph of the line.

This is not a function, as a vertical line here passes through two places on the graph of the ellipse.

(continued)

The vertical line test also can be used to explain why a vertical line is not a function.

Problems, 45. Is the Equation a Function?

Is the equation a function?

1. $y = x^2$

2. $y = x + 3$

3. $y^2 = x^2 + 4$

4. $x + y^4 = 5$

5. $y + 6 = x^3$

46. Doing Function Problems as "Function Machines"

A function is like a machine. In a gum ball machine, you put something (a coin) in, and you get something (a gum ball) out. In a function machine, you put a number in and you get the answer to a problem out.

- The function machine looks like this: F (X) = $2x + 3$

The F (X) on the left of "=" tells you the machine's name. It's called "F-machine".

F (X) .　　(X) here means "machine." **It's *not* a variable.**

↑

"F" tells the letter name of the machine.

The letter "F" and the word "machine" form the full name "F-machine."

F (X) = $2x + 3$
only means: "F-machine" is $2x + 3$.

| "is" means "=" |

Example: G (X) = $3x + 7$ . . . Means G-machine is $3x + 7$

Example: H (X) = $2x + 9$ . . . Means H-machine is $2x + 9$

- A full problem might look like this:
If G (X) = $7x + 10$, find G (4).

This means: If G-machine is $7x + 10$, what do you get when you put 4 into the machine everywhere the machine has a variable x?
　　　　G-machine is $7x + 10$
　　　　Put 4 in: 7 (4) + 10
　　　　which equals: 28 + 10
　　　　which equals: 38
　　　　When you put a 4 into this G-machine, you get 38 out.

If R (X) = $7x + 10$, find R (2).

This means: If R-machine is $7x + 10$ and you put a 2 into the variable, you get 7 (2) + 10

14 + 10

= 24

| *Note:* When you put the number into the machine, put ( ) around the number. |

If R (X) = $x^2 + x$, find R (3).

This means: If R-machine is $x^2 + x$, when 3 is put into the machine for **all** the x variables, you get

$(3)^2 + (3)$

9 + 3

= 12

| In addition to meaning "machine" the (X) in R (X) = $x^2 + x$ tells you that you're plugging in for the x variable. For a function machine like A (X) = $xy + 3y$, the (X) tells you to plug in for the x variable only. |

Problems, 46. Doing Function Problems as "Function Machines"

Use the function-machine method to solve the following:

1. If F (X) = $5x + 1$, find F (2).

2. If F (X) = $2x + 3$, find F (8).

3. If G (X) = $x + 1$, find G (4).

4. If H (X) = $x^2 + x + 1$, find H (2).

5. If S (X) = $x^2 - 2$, find S (–2).

47. More "Function Machines"

Prerequisite: FOIL method (page 14).

Example: If H (X) = x^2 + 7, find H (a + 2).

This means: If H-machine is x^2 + 7, what do you get when you put (a + 2) into the machine for every x-variable?

H-machine is	x^2 + 7
Put (a + 2) into the variable:	$(a + 2)^2$ + 7
which equals:	(a + 2) (a + 2) + 7
	a^2 + 2a + 2a + 4 + 7
	a^2 + 4a + 11

> Notice how squaring a ( )
> turned into two ( ).

When you put an (a + 2) into this H-machine, you get a^2 + 4a + 11. You can write:

$$H (a + 2) = a^2 + 4a + 11$$

which reads: "H-machine, when (a + 2) is put in, makes a^2 + 4a + 11."

Example: If G (T) = $(t + 3)^2$ + 2, find G (a + 5).

• In this problem, the variable is t, instead of x, so plug in for t.

The problem means: If G-machine = $(t + 3)^2$ + 2, and you put (a + 5) in for every variable t, what do you get out?

G-machine is	$(t + 3)^2$ + 2
Put in (a + 5):	$(a + 5 + 3)^2$ + 2
5 + 3 = 8:	$(a + 8)^2$ + 2
Square the ( ):	(a + 8) (a + 8) + 2
FOIL method (page 14):	a^2 + 8a + 8a + 64 + 2
Combine:	a^2 + 16a + 66

So when you put (a + 5) into the G-machine of $(t + 3)^2$ + 2, you get out the answer of a^2 + 16a + 66.

This can be written as G (a + 5) = a^2 + 16a + 66.

This means that putting (a + 5) into the G-machine gives you a^2 + 16a + 66.

         The You Can Do It! Guide to Algebra

Problems, 47. More "Function Machines"

Use the function-machine method to solve the following:

1. If H (X) = x^2 + 4, find H $(a + 1)$

2. If G (X) = x^2 + 2x + 1, find G (2).

3. If G (T) = $[t + 1]$, find G $(a + b)$.

4. If F (X) = $x + y$, find F (3).

5. If F (X) = $(x - 1)^2$, find F $(g + 2)$.

The You Can Do It! Guide to Algebra

48. Domain and Range

Domain is all the possible *x*-value solutions to an equation.

Range is all the possible *y*-value solutions to an equation.

You can remember that **domain**, **range** correspond to *x*, *y* (alphabetical order).

Usually, domain and range equal the real numbers, except in certain cases where restrictions apply. In problems with square roots, powers, and fraction denominators, there can be restricted answers to the domain and range.

Square Roots

The least possible square root is the square root of 0. There is no "real" solution to, say, the square root of –5. So whenever you get a domain/range problem with a square root, take what's **inside** the square root and say it must be ≥ 0. This will give you your restricted solution.

Example: $y + 5 = \sqrt{2x + 1}$ .... $2x + 1 \geq 0$
$$2x \geq -1$$
$$x \geq -\tfrac{1}{2} \text{ (Domain answer)}$$

The left side of the equation above equals **the result of a square root** from the right side of the equation. Since the possible results of a square root also must be ≥ 0, take the left side of the equation, and set it ≥ 0.
$$y + 5 \geq 0$$
$$y \geq -5 \text{ is the range.}$$

Powers

If a problem has a variable raised to an even positive power, then the result will be ≥ 0. For example, no matter what you plug into *x*, the result is always positive. This has to be taken into account for domain/range problems.

Example: $y = x^2 + 3$.

You can plug anything into the *x* [Domain: $x =$ R (real numbers)]; there is no restriction at all. But each square of what you plug in will be 0 and greater. For example, plugging in 0 results in $0 \times 0 = 0$, plugging in –2 results in $-2 \times -2 = 4$. The results start at 0 and get larger. When 3 is added to this spread of ≥ 0 numbers, the new spread will be 3 and greater (≥ 3). So $y \geq 3$. (Range: $y \geq 3$).

Denominators of Fractions

No fraction can have 0 as its denominator. So if a variable is in the denominator of an equation, you must take the whole denominator and say "This denominator $\neq 0$" and solve. This will give you your restriction on that variable.

(continued)

Example: $y = \dfrac{4}{3x + 1}$ The denominator $3x + 1$ cannot equal 0.

So:

$3x + 1 \neq 0$

$3x \neq -1$

$x \neq \dfrac{-1}{3}$ (Domain = Real numbers, except $^{-1}/_3$

Or you could say domain is $x \neq {}^{-1}/_3$)

To find range, solve for x . $y = \dfrac{4}{(3x + 1)}$ . . . $(3x +1)\,(y) = 4$ . . . $3xy + y = 4$

$3xy = 4 - y$ . . . $x = \dfrac{(4 - y)}{y}$ . . . Denominator $y \neq 0$. Range: $r, y \neq 0$.

Problems, 48. Domain and Range

Find the domain and the range:

1. $y = x^2 - 2$

2. $y = \dfrac{1}{(x + 2)}$

3. $y + 1 = \sqrt{(4x + 4)}$

4. $y = x^4 + x^2 + 4$

5. $y = \dfrac{1}{(x^2 + 4)}$

49. Variation Problems

There are three kinds of variation problems: direct variation, indirect (or inverse) variation, and joint variation.

- A typical **direct-variation** problem is phrased, "y varies directly as x." The word "varies" means "=."

    The standard form is $y = \dfrac{k \text{ (direct variables)}}{\text{(indirect variables)}}$.

    For example, "y varies **directly** as x and t" would look like:
    $$y = \frac{k(x)(t)}{1}$$

- A typical **indirect-variation** problem is phrased "y varies **indirectly** as m and n would look like:
    $$y = \frac{k}{(m)(n)}$$

- **Joint variation** has both direct and indirect (also called inverse) variables. For example, "y varies jointly (which means **directly**) as x and t and inversely as a" would look like:
    $$y = \frac{k(x)(t)}{(a)}$$

Solving Problems

- Read the first sentence and set up the equation.

- Then you'll be given the value of **every variable except** k. Plug in the first set of values you are given, and solve for k.

- After solving for k, start over with your equation, and plug in the second set of values given, and plug in k, too. Then solve for the unknown letter.

    Example: "y varies **directly** as x. {If $y = 10$ when $x = 2$}, find {y when $x = 6$}.

    The first set of values is $y = 10$ and $x = 2$. The second set of values is $x = 6$.

Set up the equation:	$y = k\ (x)$
Plug in the first set of values:	$(10) = k\ (2)$
	$10 = 2k$
	$k = 10 \div 2 = 5$
Repeat the original equation:	$y = k\ (x)$
Plug in the second set of values, and plug in k:	$y = (5)\ (6)$
	$y = 30$
y varies directly as the square of x:	$y = k\ (x^2)$
y varies directly as the cube of x^3:	$y = k\ (x^3)$

   The You Can Do It! Guide to Algebra

Problems, 49. *Variation Problems*

Write as an equation or solve:

1. y varies directly as m and n.

2. y varies jointly (directly) as a and indirectly as b and c.

3. y varies directly as x and indirectly as z.

4. y varies directly as x^2. If y is 16 when x is 2, find y when x is 4.

5. y varies jointly (directly) as a and b and indirectly as c. If y is 1 when a is 1, b is 2, and c is 4, find y when a is 4, b is 2, and c is 4.

50. Symmetry and Degree

Symmetry

There are three different symmetries to test for: x-axis, y-axis, and both-axes.

x-**axis** symmetry: Plug in a positive y-value and its negative opposite (like 2 and –2). If you get the same x-value out, the graph has x-axis symmetry.

y-**axis** symmetry: Plug in a positive x-value and its negative opposite (like 2 and –2). If you get the same y-value out each time, the graph has y-axis symmetry.

Both-axes symmetry: Plug in a positive x-value and its negative opposite (like 2 and –2). If the results yield opposites of the same number (like 2 and –2), it's symmetric to both axes.

$y = x^2$

Test for x-axis symmetry:	Plugging in 4 for y gives us x = 2 or –2.
	Plugging in –4 for y gives us no solution.
Test for y-axis symmetry:	Plugging in 4 for x gives y =16. ←
	Plugging in –4 for x gives y =16. ←
Test both–axes symmetry:	Plugging in 2 for x gives 4.
	Plugging in –2 for x gives 4.

The same y-value results! This means the graph has y-symmetry.

The graph is symmetric to the y-axis only.

$y = x$

Test for x-axis symmetry:	Plugging in 4 for y gives us x = 4.
	Plugging in –4 for y gives us x = –4.
Test for y-axis symmetry:	Plugging in 3 for x gives y = 3.
	Plugging in 3 for x gives y = –3.
Test for both-axes symmetry:	Plugging in 2 for x gives y = 2. ←
	Plugging in –2 for x gives y = –2. ←

The positive 2 and negative 2 for x-values give "the same" opposite of the same number (2). Both-axes symmetry!

This graph is symmetric to both axes.

Degree

For degree, if a letter variable has no exponent, give it an exponent of 1. Then add up all the powers **of the letter variables only**. This gives you the degree of the term. For example:

$x^3 y^2 z^4$ has a degree of 9.

$4^3 x^3 y^2 z^4$ also has a degree of 9 (only add the **letters'** exponents).

xy has a degree of 2 (each letter variable gets an exponent of 1).

The **degree of an expression** is the highest degree of any term in it. So $xy + x^3 y^2 z^4$ has a degree of 9 (from the right-hand term).

     The You Can Do It! Guide to Algebra

Problems, 50. Symmetry and Degree

Test for symmetry:

1. $y = x^2 + 1$

2. $x = y^2 + 1$

3. $x = 2$

4. $y = 4$

Find the degree:

5. $2^2 a^2 b^2 c^2 d^1$

51. Exponent Rules

Rule 1. **Multiply means add**: When multiplying two things, add the exponents from the same variables (letters) or the same numbers.

$$x^2 \times x^4 = x^6 \qquad\qquad a^2 b^4 \times a^1 b^4 = a^3 b^8$$

Rule 2. **Divide means subtract**: When dividing two terms, subtract downward the exponents from the same variables or numbers. The results go on the top of the fraction bar.

$$\frac{x^6}{x^2} = x^4 \qquad\qquad \frac{2x^2}{x^4} = \frac{2x^{-2}}{1} = \frac{2}{x^2}$$

Rule 3. **Parentheses means multiply**: If there is **multiplication and division only** (no addition or subtraction) inside the parentheses, then multiply the exponent outside the parentheses times **every exponent** of every letter and number inside the parentheses. If a letter or number has no exponent, give it an exponent of 1.

$$\left(\frac{4x^3 y^9 z^2}{a^2 b^4} \right)^2 \qquad \text{Remember: 4 here is really } 4^1.$$

$$= \frac{4^2 x^6 y^{18} z^4}{a^4 b^8} \qquad \text{You can convert } 4^2 \text{ to 16.}$$

Rule 4. **A letter or number raised to a negative exponent** changes sides of the fraction bar and its exponent changes its sign. If there's nothing remaining on one side of the fraction, put a 1.

$$\frac{y}{x^{-3}} = \frac{yx^3}{1}$$

Another example: $\dfrac{x^{-6}}{x^2} = \dfrac{1}{x^2 x^6} = \dfrac{1}{x^8}$

Rule 5. **Anything raised to the 0 exponent equals 1.**

$$5^0 = 1 \qquad x^0 = 1 \qquad \left(\frac{x^2 y^2 z^6}{6} \right)^0 = 1$$

Rule 6. **An addition or subtraction sign in a problem nullifies almost every rule.**

$$(x^6 + y^4)^2 \neq x^{12} y^8$$

Rule 7. **An exponent only raises the letter or number it is a power of, unless it is raising a whole parentheses.** *Example:* $3x^2$, which is really $3^1 x^2$.

Problems, 51. Exponent Rules

Solve the following:

1. $y^3 \times y^5$

2. $\dfrac{x^6}{x^3}$

3. $\dfrac{x^{-10}}{x^4}$

4. $(4z)^0$

5. $(x^2 + y^2)^2$

Graphs of Conic Sections

52. Parabolas (pa-`ra-bol-lahs)

Parabola equations have only one squared variable (either x^2 or y^2).

Examples:

$$y = x^2 + 9 \qquad x \text{ is the squared variable.}$$
$$x = 4y^2 + 3 \qquad y \text{ is the squared variable.}$$
$$2y^2 = x \qquad y \text{ is the squared variable.}$$
$$x^2 + y + 4x + 4 = 0 \qquad x \text{ is the squared variable.}$$

The graph of a parabola "opens" left, right, up, or down.

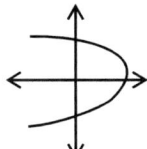 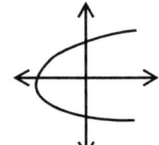 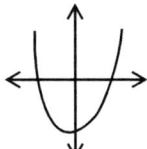 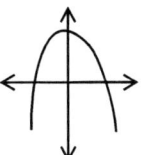

Step 1. Find the vertex from the equation.

- Move all terms containing the unsquared variable to one side. Put everything else on the other side of the equal sign.

- Divide everything through by the variable's coefficient so the equation becomes $y = \ldots$ or $x = \ldots$

$$x^2 + y + 4x + 4 = 0$$
$$y = -x^2 - 4x - 4$$

> Here, x is the squared variable and y is the unsquared variable.

Step 2. From the squared variable side, get a, b, and c coefficients as in the quadratic formula.

$$a = -1 \quad b = -4 \quad c = -4$$

Step 3. Plug a and b into . . . $\dfrac{-b}{2a} = \dfrac{-(-4)}{2(-1)} = \dfrac{4}{-2} = -2$

Step 4. Put the answer into a table (under the squared variable column).

x	y
-2	0

Step 5. Substitute the answer into the equation, and solve for the other variable.

$$y = -(-2)^2 - 4(-2) - 4$$
$$y = -(4) + 8 - 4$$

$y = 0$. Put this value into the table now. The point $(-2, 0)$ is the vertex point.

(continued)

Step 6. Plug in for the squared variable a number that is one greater than the squared variable (here, the squared variable is x) vertex value and one less than this value.

for $x = -1$ (one greater than -2) $x = -3$ (one less than -2)

$y = -(-1)^2 - 4(-1) - 4$ $y = -(-3)^2 - 4(-3) - 4$

$y = -(1) + 4 - 4 \ldots = -1$ $y = -9 + 12 - 4 = -1$

$(-1, -1)$ $(-3, -1)$

x	y
-2	0
-1	-1
-3	-1

Step 7. Graph the points and draw the parabola.

Problems, 52. Parabolas

Graph the following:

1. $y = x^2$

2. $y = x^2 + 4$

3. $y = -2x^2$

4. $y = x^2 + 4x + 4$

5. $y = 5x^2 + 1$

53. Parabolas: Completing the Square

Prerequisite: Parabolas (page 111).

Follow these steps to solve for the graph of a parabola by "completing the square" and factoring:

Step 1. Keep the squared variable and terms with this squared variable in them, on the left side of the equation. Leave some space as shown. Move all other terms to the right side of the equation.

$$y^2 - 4y - 8x - 28 \quad = 0$$
$$y^2 - 4y \quad\quad\quad = 8x + 28$$

Step 2. Complete the square on the left side.

Half of –4 is –2.
–2 × –2 = 4.
Add 4 to the right side.

$$y^2 - \mathbf{4}y = 8x + 28$$
$$(y - \mathbf{2})^2 = 8x + 28 + \mathbf{4}$$
$$(y - 2)^2 = 8x + 32 \quad \ldots [28 + 4 = 32]$$

Step 3. Factor the right side of the equation, and stop.

$$y^2 - 4y \quad = 8x + 32$$
$$(y - 2)^2 \quad = 8\,(x + 4)$$

Step 4. Take each parentheses separately, say it is equal to 0, and solve.

$$(y - 2)^2 \quad = 8\,(x + 4)$$
$$y - 2 = 0 \quad x + 4 = 0$$
$$y = 2 \quad\quad x = -4$$

The (x,y) vertex point is (–4, 2).

x	y
–4	2

Step 5. Solve as in Step 5 from Parabolas (page 111).

One below $y = 2$, is $y = 1$
$$(1 - 2)^2 = 8\,(x + 4)$$
$$(-1)^2 = 8x + 32$$
$$1 = 8x + 32$$
$$1 - 32 = 8x$$
$$-31 = 8x$$
$$x = {}^{-31}/_8$$

One above $y = 2$, is $y = 3$
$$(3 - 2) = 8\,(x + 4)$$
$$(1) = 8x + 32$$
$$1 = 8x + 32$$
$$1 - 32 = 8x$$
$$-31 = 8x$$
$$x = {}^{-31}/_8$$

x	y
–4	2
–31/8	1
–31/8	3

Finding the directrix:
Use the **directrix** formula:
"The squared variable = its vertex value."
So y (the squared variable) = 2 (y-value from vertex) . . . $y = 2$ is the directrix.

1 2 3 4 5

Problems, 53. Parabolas: Completing the Square

Complete the square, and solve and graph the parabola:

1. $x^2 + 4x = y - 2$

2. $x^2 - 2x - y = 1$

3. $y^2 + 6x = x - 6$

4. $y^2 - 4y = x - 6$

5. $x^2 + 2x = y - 5$

54. Circles

The standard form of a circle with a center at (0,0) is:

$$x^2 + y^2 = (\text{radius})^2$$

Example:
$$x^2 + y^2 = 16$$
$$x^2 + y^2 = (4)^2 \quad (\text{because } 16 = 4 \times 4)$$
The radius is 4.

Put points four units left, right, up, and down from the center (0,0) and make a circle.

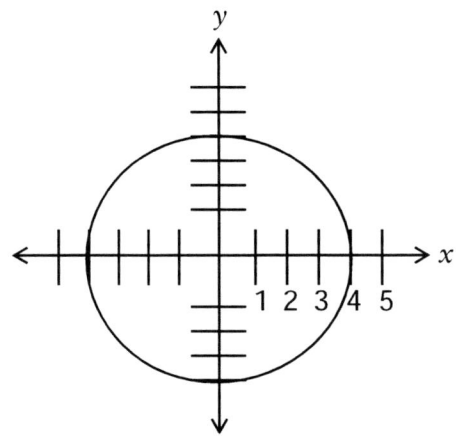

But sometimes the center is not at (0,0). Then the equation standard form is:

$$(x - h)^2 + (y - k)^2 = (\text{radius})^2$$

Example: $\quad (x - 3)^2 + (y+2)^2 = 4$

Step 1. Take each parentheses separately, say it is equal to 0, and solve.

$$x - 3 = 0 \qquad\qquad y + 2 = 0$$
$$x = 3 \qquad\qquad\quad y = -2$$

• The center is at (3, –2).

Step 2. Find the radius by getting the square root of the number on the right side of the equation.

The radius is the square root of 4, which is 2.

• Go two left, right, up, and down from the center point (3, –2), and put points. Connect the points to form a circle.

(continued)

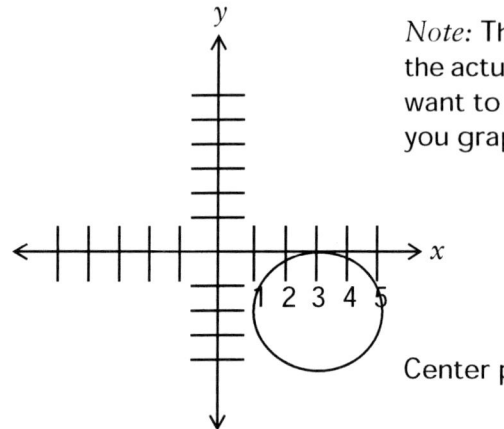

Note: The center point is **not** part of the actual circle graph. So you may not want to put the center point in when you graph circles for class.

Center point is (3, –2).

You may also encounter problems requiring completing the square in two places.

Example: $x^2 + 4x + y^2 + 6y = 3$

Complete the squares: $(x + 2)^2 + (y + 3)^2 = 3 + 4 + 9$

Problems, 54. Circles

Find the center of the circle, the radius of the circle, and graph:

1. $x^2 + y^2 = 4$

2. $(x - 2)^2 + y^2 = 25$

3. $(x - 1)^2 + (y - 2)^2 = 9$

4. $(x + 4)^2 + (y - 5)^2 = 16$

5. $x^2 + 2x + y^2 + 6x = 6$

55. Ellipses (eh-lips-ees)

Ellipses are comparable to ovals.

Their standard form is: $\dfrac{x^2}{\text{number}} + \dfrac{y^2}{\text{number}} = 1$

> It must be set equal to 1.

Example:

$$\frac{x^2}{4} + \frac{y^2}{9} = 1$$

Follow these steps to graph the ellipse:

- Take the ± square roots of the x^2 denominator, and plot them on the x-axis.

- Take the ± square roots of the y^2 denominator, and plot them on the y-axis.

  The x^2 denominator is 4, its ± square roots are + 2 and –2. Plot on the x-axis.

  The y^2 denominator is 9, its ± square roots are + 3 and –3. Plot on the y-axis.

- Graph the ellipse.

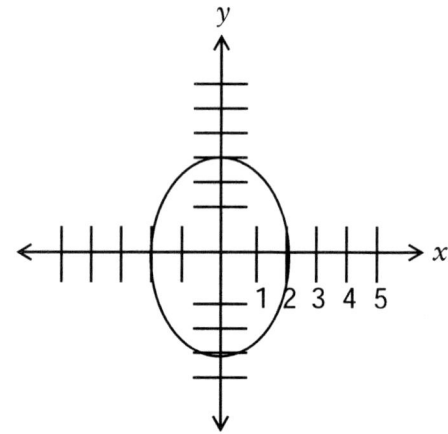

To find the "focus" (plural: "foci"): subtract denominators and take the square root.

- Take the greater denominator (here y).

- Add/subtract the square root to/from that value's coordinate in (0,0).
  9 – 4 = 5, so **(0, 0 + √5), (0, 0 – √5)**.

(continued)

You may have to move terms around and divide through to get a 1.

$$12x^2 + 3y^2 = 12$$

$$\frac{\overset{1}{\cancel{12}}x^2}{\underset{1}{\cancel{12}}} + \frac{\overset{1}{\cancel{3}}y^2}{\underset{4}{\cancel{12}}} = \frac{\overset{1}{\cancel{12}}}{\underset{1}{\cancel{12}}}$$

Divide everything through by 12 to get the right side number to equal 1. Cancel fractions.

$$\frac{x^2}{1} + \frac{y^2}{4} = 1$$

The x^2 denominator is 1, its ± square roots are + 1 and –1. Plot on the x-axis.

The y^2 denominator is 4, its ± square roots are + 2 and –2. Plot on the y-axis.

Graph the ellipse.

Foci: 4 – 1 = 3 so (0, 0 + √3), (0, 0 – √3)

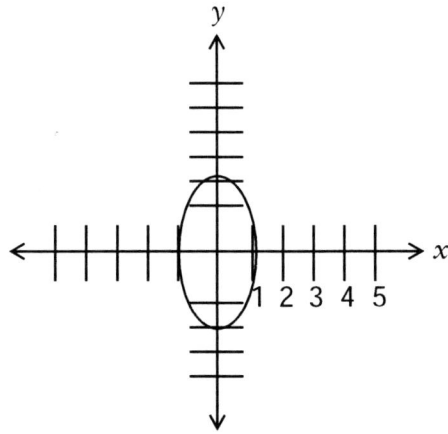

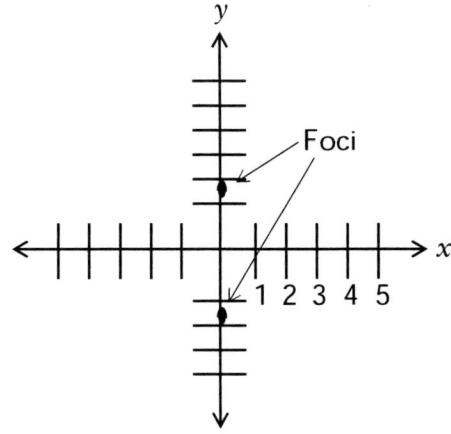

Problems, 55. Ellipses

Solve and graph the ellipse. State where points lie on the x and y axes.

1. $\dfrac{x^2}{16} + \dfrac{y^2}{4} = 1$

2. $\dfrac{x^2}{25} + \dfrac{y^2}{36} = 1$

3. $4x^2 + 16y^2 = 16$

4. $x^2 + 25y^2 = 625$

5. $5x^2 + 20y^2 = 80$

 The You Can Do It! Guide to Algebra

56. Hyperbolas (hi-`per-boh-lahs)

The graphs of hyperbolas look like parabolas opening in opposite directions:

Hyperbola standard form: $\dfrac{x^2}{\text{number}} - \dfrac{y^2}{\text{number}} = 1$

Where the ellipse equation had a + between fractions, the hyperbola has a –.

Example: $\dfrac{x^2}{4} - \dfrac{y^2}{9} = 1$

To plot points, use the same process as with ellipses.

- Take the ± square roots of the x^2 denominator, and plot them on the x-axis.

- Take the ± square roots of the y^2 denominator, and plot them on the y-axis.

The x^2 denominator is 4, its ± square roots are + 2 and –2. Plot on the x-axis.

The y^2 denominator is 9, its ± square roots are + 3 and –3. Plot on the y-axis.

- Make a rectangular box out of these points. Draw diagonal lines through the box corners.

- Take the first fraction's variable letter (here, x). Graph two parabolas off this variable's axis.

- Graph along the outlines of the box and diagonals, and out into space. Then erase the box and the diagonals.

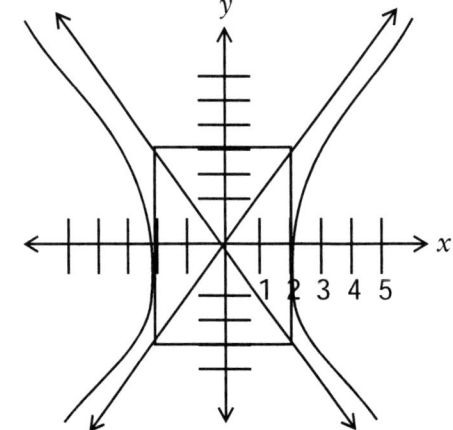

Foci: Add the denominators, and take the square root. 4 + 9 = 13, so $\sqrt{13}$

- Take the first fractions's variable letter (here, an x).

- Add/subtract the square root to/from this variable's values in the vertex points of your hyperbola drawings.

Example: The vertex points were (2, 0) and (–2, 0). Add $\sqrt{13}$ to the positive x coordinate and subtract $\sqrt{13}$ from the negative x coordinate (here, –3).

- The foci are (2 + $\sqrt{13}$, 0) and (–2 – $\sqrt{13}$, 0).

The You Can Do It! Guide to Algebra

Problems, 56. Hyperbolas

Solve and graph the hyperbola:

1. $\dfrac{x^2}{100} - \dfrac{y^2}{64} = 1$

2. $\dfrac{x^2}{1} - \dfrac{y^2}{25} = 1$

3. $4x^2 - 16y^2 = 16$

4. $10x^2 - 40y^2 = 10$

5. $5x^2 - 20y^2 = 80$

Square Roots and Logarithms

57. Square Roots

Here's a square root sign: $\sqrt{}$

A square root sign will contain a number: $\sqrt{25}$

Follow these steps to find the square root of the number:

Step 1. Break down the number inside the square root sign into prime factors. For example, $25 = 5 \times 5$, and $12 = 2 \times \mathbf{6} = 2 \times \mathbf{3} \times \mathbf{2}$. Avoid using 1's as factors.

Step 2. Rewrite the square root sign with the factors inside it.
$$\sqrt{25} = \sqrt{5 \times 5}$$

Step 3. Look for **identical factors**. Since this problem is a **square** root, look for two identical factors. Above, they are 5 and 5.

Step 4. Circle the same factors. Here, 5 and 5.

Step 5. Cross out the circled factors, and write **only one** of these circled factors outside of the square root.

5 $\sqrt{5 \times 5}$

Step 6. Return to Step 3 and look for other identical factors. Here, there are none, so proceed to Step 7.

Step 7. Multiply all the numbers that are now outside of the square root. Here there is just a 5, so there is no multiplication.

Step 8. If factors remain inside the square root sign, leave them and you have an answer (erase the factors that were circled and crossed out). If no factors remain inside the square root sign, erase it and everything else inside it (the factors that were circled and crossed out, the circles, the cross-outs, etc.). Here, the answer is 5 after you erase the square root sign, etc.

Example: $\sqrt{12} = \sqrt{4 \times 3} = \sqrt{2 \times 2 \times 3}$

Answer: $2\sqrt{3}$

Problems, 57. Square Roots

Find the square root of the following:

1. $\sqrt{20}$

2. $\sqrt{18}$

3. $\sqrt{16}$

4. $\sqrt{36}$

5. $\sqrt{50}$

58. Square Roots, a Chart, and Fraction Exponents

Prerequisite: Square Roots, page 123.

Here is a useful chart of numbers and exponents frequently found in home-work problems:

$2^2 = 4$	$3^2 = 9$	$4^2 = 16$	$5^2 = 25$	$6^2 = 36$
$2^3 = 8$	$3^3 = 27$	$4^3 = 64$	$5^3 = 125$	$6^3 = 216$
$2^4 = 16$	$3^4 = 81$	$4^4 = 256$	$5^4 = 625$	
$2^5 = 32$	$3^5 = 243$			
$2^6 = 64$				
$2^7 = 128$				
$2^8 = 256$				
$2^9 = 512$				

- An exponent of a number indicates how many times the number is to be multiplied by itself.

  Example: 3^4 = four threes, multiplied together = $3 \times 3 \times 3 \times 3 = 81$.

- A fraction exponent, or fraction power, is solved by working with square roots.

  Example: $16^{\frac{1}{2}}$ (16 raised to the $\frac{1}{2}$ power).

  ⟵ the whole number

Step 1. Put the whole number inside a square root sign.

$$\sqrt{16}$$

Step 2. Raise the whole number to the fraction numerator power

$$\sqrt{16^1}$$

Step 3. Place the fraction denominator outside the square root as a root sign exponent.

$$\sqrt[2]{16^1}$$

Summarizing Steps 1–3: The numerator goes **inside** the root, with the whole number raised to it. The denominator goes **outside** the root, as a root sign exponent.

Step 4. Perform the operation of the whole number raised to the power.

$$\sqrt[2]{16^1} = 16^1 = 16 \text{ -----> } \sqrt[2]{16}$$

(continued)

Step 5. Perform all the steps necessary to get a square root answer (page 123). The root sign exponent (here, 2) tells you how many of the group of identical factors to circle in the circling step (here, circle groups of two identical factors).

Problems, 58. Square Roots, a Chart, and Fraction Exponents

Solve the following fraction-exponent problems by working with square roots:

1. $9^{\frac{1}{2}}$

2. $25^{\frac{1}{2}}$

3. $18^{\frac{1}{2}}$

4. $50^{\frac{1}{2}}$

5. $27^{\frac{1}{3}}$

59. More Square Roots and Fraction Exponents

Follow the steps below to solve a fraction exponent problem when the numerator of the fraction is 1:

Example: $16^{\frac{1}{4}} = \sqrt[4]{16^1}$

Step 1. Break down $16 = 8 \times 2 = 4 \times 2 \times 2 = 2 \times 2 \times 2 \times 2$.

Step 2. Circle and cross out four identical number factors. Write one of the factors outside the square root. Cross out the square root sign.

$2 \ \sqrt[4]{2 \times 2 \times 2 \times 2}$

Answer: 2.

The numerator of a fraction exponent may be greater than 1. Here are two ways to solve the following problem:

$$16^{\frac{3}{4}} = \sqrt[4]{16^3}$$

Method 1

Step 1. Expand $16^3 = 16 \times 16 \times 16$

Step 2. $16 = 2 \times 2 \times 2 \times 2$; $16 = 2 \times 2 \times 2 \times 2$; $16 = 2 \times 2 \times 2 \times 2$

Step 3. $2, 2, 2 \ \sqrt[4]{2 \times 2 \times 2 \times 2 \times 2 \times 2 \times 2 \times 2 \times 2 \times 2 \times 2 \times 2}$

Answer: $2 \times 2 \times 2 = 8$.

Method 2

$$16^{\frac{3}{4}} = \sqrt[4]{16^3}$$

Step 1. Break down $16 = 2 \times 2 \times 2 \times 2$.

Step 2. $\sqrt[4]{(2 \times 2 \times 2 \times 2)^3}$

Step 3. $2 \ \sqrt[4]{(2 \times 2 \times 2 \times 2)^3}$

Step 4. Now expand 2 to the ^{3} power.

Step 5. $2^3 = 8$

Answer: 8

(continued)

In the first method, the whole number was raised to the power first, then broken down, and circled in groups of four identical numbers. One identical number was removed from each group and written outside the square root sign.

In the second method, the number was broken down, and the factors were circled. Then the removed factor was raised to the power to get the final answer.

Problems, 59. More Square Roots and Fraction Exponents

Solve the following fraction-exponent problems:

1. $8^{\frac{1}{3}}$

2. $9^{\frac{3}{2}}$

3. $27^{\frac{2}{3}}$

4. $25^{\frac{3}{2}}$

5. $64^{\frac{5}{6}}$

60. Getting Rid of Square Roots in Denominators

No Square Roots Allowed!

A square root answer cannot have a square root in a fraction denominator. To get rid of this square root in a denominator in a flash:

- Write the denominator's square root in the numerator.

- Erase the denominator's square root sign (leaving the whole number).

$$\frac{1}{\sqrt{2}} = \frac{1\sqrt{2}}{\sqrt{2}} = \frac{1\sqrt{2}}{\sqrt{2}} = \frac{1\sqrt{2}}{2}$$

Erase root sign

Rationalizing the Denominator When the Root Sign Exponent > 2

Example:

$$\frac{1}{\sqrt[3]{2}}$$

Step 1. The root sign exponent tells you how many identical whole numbers you need to circle, using the technique stated on the first square roots page, page 123, (or any method you would like to use to take the root).

Step 2. Multiply times however many numbers you need in a fraction that includes the same square root sign and numbers in its numerator and denominator.

$$\frac{1}{\sqrt[3]{2}} \times \frac{\sqrt[3]{2 \times 2}}{\sqrt[3]{2 \times 2}} = \frac{1\sqrt[3]{2 \times 2}}{\sqrt[3]{2 \times 2 \times 2}}$$

- Because two more 2's are needed to make a group of three in the denominator.

$$\frac{1\sqrt[3]{4}}{2\sqrt[3]{2 \times 2 \times 2}} = \frac{\sqrt[3]{4}}{2}$$

Multiplying by the Conjugate

Here is how to eliminate square roots from denominators that look like this:

$$\sqrt{2} + 3 \qquad \sqrt{2} - 3 \qquad 2 + \sqrt{3} \qquad 2 - \sqrt{3}$$

Multiply by a fraction with the exact same denominator (only change the sign in the middle). Do the same for the numerator.

Example:

$$\frac{1}{\sqrt{2} + 3} \times \frac{\sqrt{2} - 3}{\sqrt{2} - 3} = \frac{\sqrt{2} - 3}{\sqrt{4} - 3\sqrt{2} + 3\sqrt{2} - 9} = \frac{\sqrt{2} - 3}{2 - 9} = \frac{\sqrt{2} - 3}{-7}$$

Problems, 60. Getting Rid of Square Roots in Denominators

Eliminate the square roots from the denominators in these fractions:

1. $\dfrac{1}{\sqrt{3}}$

2. $\dfrac{2}{\sqrt[3]{9}}$

3. $\dfrac{1}{\sqrt{3}+2}$

4. $\dfrac{4}{\sqrt{5}}$

5. $\dfrac{5}{\sqrt[3]{25}}$

61. Adding, Subtracting, and Multiplying Square Roots

Before we add, subtract, and multiply square roots, let's review some basics. Here's how to find square roots:

Examples:

$$\sqrt{36} \quad 36 = 9 \times 4 = 3 \times 3 \times 4 = 3 \times 3 \times 2 \times 2$$

$$3, 2 \ \sqrt{3 \times 3} \times \overline{2 \times 2}$$

Answer: $3 \times 2 = 6.$

$$5\sqrt{49} \quad \sqrt{49} = 7 \times 7$$

$$7, 5 \ \sqrt{7 \times 7}$$

Answer: $7 \times 5 = 35.$

Adding Square Roots

The numbers inside the root must be the same. Add only the outside numbers.

Example:

$$2\sqrt{5} + 3\sqrt{5} = 5\sqrt{5}.$$

> *Note:* You can only add and subtract roots that have the same "root sign" number.

The square root and whole number just go along for the ride.

Subtracting Square Roots

The numbers inside the root must be the same. Subtract only the outside numbers.

$$2\sqrt{5} - 3\sqrt{5} = -1\sqrt{5}.$$

Multiplying Square Roots

Multiply outside numbers, and separately, multiply inside numbers. "Outside product" goes outside; "inside product" goes inside the square root.

$$2\sqrt{5} \times 4\sqrt{7} = 8\sqrt{35}.$$

> $2 \times 4 = 8$, and
> $5 \times 7 = 35.$

(continued)

Combining When Root Sign Numbers Are Different

The numbers inside the root signs in the following example are different. To combine the square roots, break down numbers, circle, and cross out until you get like roots.

$$5\sqrt{27} + 2\sqrt{3} - 4\sqrt{75}$$

$$5\sqrt{(3 \times 3) \times 3} + 2\sqrt{3} - 4\sqrt{(5 \times 5) \times 3}$$

$$3, 5\sqrt{(3 \times 3) \times 3} + 2\sqrt{3} - 4, 5\sqrt{(5 \times 5) \times 3}$$

| $27 = 3 \times 3 \times 3$ |
| $75 = 5 \times 5 \times 3$ |

$$15\sqrt{3} + 2\sqrt{3} - 20\sqrt{3}$$

Answer: $-3\sqrt{3}$

> Now all numbers inside roots are the same (all 3). Adding the outsides of 15, 2, and –20 equals –3.

Problems, 61. Adding, Subtracting, and Multiplying Square Roots

Combine the following square roots:

1. $2\sqrt{3} + 5\sqrt{3}$

2. $4\sqrt{5} - 2\sqrt{5}$

3. $\sqrt{72} - \sqrt{50} + \sqrt{18}$

4. $\sqrt{45} + \sqrt{20} - \sqrt{125}$

5. $-\sqrt{24} + \sqrt{6} + \sqrt{54}$

62. Logarithm Rules

Logarithm Form

- The word "log" has a "base" number to the right and below it.

- At the same level as "log" and after the base is a real number or variable, then an equal sign.

- To the right of the equal sign is a real number or variable.

$$\log_{10} 100 = 2$$

- You can call the number on the left side of the equal sign the "near number."

- You can call the number on the right side of the equal sign the "far number."

$$\log_{10} 100 = 2$$

the word "log" base near number far number

Rule #1. Exponential Form

base$^{\text{far number}}$ = near number

From the example above: $10^2 = 100$ (10 is the base, 2 is far, 100 is near.)

A typical question might ask: What is $\log_4 16$?

To solve this, set it $= x$: $\log_4 16 = x$ (What the log equals is unknown.)

Then apply Rule #1 (base to the far equals near).

$$4^x = 16$$

4 raised to ? makes 16. 4 raised to **the second power** equals 16. So $x = 2$.

Rule #2. The Product Rule

log $(a \times b)$ = log a + log b

One log, doing multiplication, becomes many logs, doing addition.

Examples: log (2×5) = log 2 + log 5 . . . vice versa . . . log a + log b = log ab

(continued)

Rule #3. The Quotient Rule

$$\log \frac{x}{y} = \log x - \log y$$

One log, doing division, becomes many logs formed of the numerators (all stay positive) minus the denominators.

Examples: $\log \dfrac{ab}{c} = \log a + \log b - \log c$ . . . and vice versa . . .

$$\log a + \log b - \log c = \log \frac{ab}{c}$$

Rule #4. The Log 1 Rule

$$\log 1 = 0$$

The log of 1, regardless of base, always equals 0.

Examples: $\log_4 1 = 0 \quad \log_{12} 1 = 0 \quad \log_x 1 = 0$

Rule #5. The Power Rule

$$\log 10^2 = 2 \log 10$$

If the value after "log" is raised to a power, the power is put in front of "log."

Examples: $\log 22^4 = 4 \log 22$ . . . and vice versa . . . $2 \log 5 = \log 5^2$

Log problems summary: If it's condensed, expand it. If it's expanded, condense it.

Problems, 62. Logarithm Rules

Solve the following:

1. $\log_8 64 = x$

2. $\log_6 1 = x$

3. True or false: $\log_{10} 100 = 2$

4. True or false: $\log_5 25 = 2$

5. $\log_2 x = 6$

Tips

1. Go slowly, step by step. Please focus on only one step at a time.

2. Remember that it is all about understanding. If you *don't* understand it, how can it not be hard? If you *do* understand it, how can it not be easy?

3. You can do it!

4. Find someone who has successfully gone through the class, to give yourself a positive role model to follow.

5. Find a tutor or student who will help you when you need it. If you're stressed or need a lot of help, don't ask close friends or prospective friends to tutor you. Get help from a professional, and keep your friends your friends.

6. Ask questions; that gives you understanding. Use school to your advantage.

7. Do your homework as if you were doing a test. Get in the habit of writing neatly, etc.

8. You can take a class as many times as you need to, which is far superior to cheating.

9. Math is mostly mental exercise, like phys ed for the brain. Remember to detach yourself from the struggle, and remember math's function in your life.

10. If you don't understand something, seek out a better explanation that you *can* understand. Try to rephrase a new concept in terms of something you already understand.

11. Don't spend too much time talking about math with unsympathetic people.

12. There are different levels of math classes. Look for the best class for you. Classes that assign homework help your understanding, because you will have to be more involved.

13. If you have a problem with your teacher, talk to your teacher about it.

Answers to Problems

1. Combining Positive and Negative Numbers, page 2:
   1. 5
   2. 5
   3. –2
   4. 3
   5. –7

2. Moving Terms Across the Equal Sign, page 4:
   1. $x = 5 - 2$
   2. $x = 14 + 12$
   3. $x = 6 + 2$
   4. $x = 0 + 2$
   5. $2x + 4y = 5 - 1$

3. A New Way to Do Fractions, page 6:
   1. $^7/_6$
   2. $^{-1}/_6$
   3. $^7/_{12}$
   4. $^1/_{12}$
   5. $^{33}/_{40}$

4. Reducing Fractions, page 8:
   1. $^1/_3$
   2. $^1/_4$
   3. $^2/_5$
   4. x^2
   5. x^6

5. Ratio Proportions, page 11:
   1. 64 ounces
   2. 3 $^1/_3$ flashlights
   3. 7 $^3/_5$ km

4. 45 peanut candies
5. $38.50

6. Properties and Identities, page 13:
   1. Associative property of addition
   2. Commutative property of addition
   3. Distributive property
   4. Addition of zero identity
   5. Commutative property of multiplication

7. FOIL Method, page 15:
   1. $x^2 + 7x + 12$
   2. $x^2 + 8x + 12$
   3. $x^2 + 1x - 6$
   4. $x^2 + 6x - 40$
   5. $x^2 - 7x + 12$

8. Absolute Value, page 18:
   1. $-5 > x > -3$
   2. $-3 > x > 1$
   3. $x = 2$ and $x = -10$
   4. $x < 4$ or $x > 10$
   5. $-13 < x < 3$

9. Synthetic Division, page 20:
   1. $3x + 3$
   2. $2x + 5$
   3. $x + 4$
   4. $5x + 1$
   5. $4x + 7$

10. Common Factoring: Numbers, page 22:
    1. $2 (1 + 3 + 5)$
    2. $4 (1 + 3 + 5)$
    3. $5 (3 + 2 - 5)$
    4. $4 (4 + 6 - 1)$
    5. $7 (-3 + 4 - 2)$

(continued)

11. Common Factoring: Variables, page 24:
    1. $x (1 + x^2)$
    2. $x^2 (x^2 + 1)$
    3. $x^1 y^2 (x^1 - y^1)$
    4. $x^2 y^2 z^1 (z^1 + x^2 y^1)$
    5. $a^1 (a^1 b^1 c^1 + 2b^1 + 3c^1)$

12. Common Factoring: Numbers and Variables, page 26:
    1. $2x^2 (1 + 2x^3)$
    2. $2x^3 (7 + 9x^9)$
    3. $5x^1 y^2 (x^1 - 2y^1)$
    4. $3x^2 y^2 (1 + 3x^2 y^1)$
    5. $6x^1 y^2 (2 + y^1)$

13. Factoring: Three Terms, page 29:
    1. $(x + 4) (x + 1)$
    2. $(x + 3) (x + 4)$
    3. $(x + 2) (x + 2)$
    4. $(x - 3) (x - 2)$
    5. $(x + 3) (x - 2)$

14. Factoring: Two Terms, Difference of Squares, page 31:
    1. $(x + 4) (x - 4)$
    2. $(x + 5) (x - 5)$
    3. $(x^3 + y) (x^3 - y)$
    4. $(2x + 5y^3) (2x - 5y^3)$
    5. $(y^2 + 9) (y^2 - 9)$

15. Factoring: Trial and Error Factoring, page 33:
    1. $(2x + 3) (x + 1)$
    2. $(2x + 1) (x + 7)$
    3. $(3x + 2) (x + 3)$
    4. $(2x - 1) (x + 2)$
    5. $(5x + 2) (x + 1)$

16. Factoring, Part I: The AC Coefficient Method, page 35:
    1. $(2x + 3) (x + 1)$
    2. $(2x + 3) (x + 4)$
    3. $(2x + 5) (x + 1)$
    4. $(3x + 1) (x + 2)$
    5. $(2x - 1) (x + 1)$

17. Factoring, Part II: Factoring by Grouping, page 37:
    1. $(x + 2) (x + 7)$
    2. $(x + 4) (x + 5)$
    3. $(x + 2) (x + 10)$
    4. $(x + 2) (3x + 1)$
    5. $(2x - 1) (x + 2)$

18. Factoring: Two Terms, Difference of Cubes, page 39:
    1. $(x - 4) (x^2 + 4x + 16)$
    2. $(5 + x) (25 - 5x + x^2)$
    3. $(6 - x^2) (36 + 6x^2 + x^4)$
    4. $(x - 5) (x^2 + 5x + 25)$
    5. $(3 + y^3) (9 - 3y^3 + y^6)$

19. Greatest Common Number: Factoring Tips, page 41:
    1. Yes. No.
    2. Yes. Yes.
    3. Yes. No.
    4. Yes. Yes. Yes.
    5. 2, 4, 5, 8

20. Dictionary for Word Problems, page 43:
    1. $8x + 3$
    2. $\sqrt{x} - 5$
    3. Perimeter = 12
    4. .40
    5. $5 = 3 + 2$

21. Word Problems: Age Problems, page 46:
    1. $m = j - 2$
    2. $d + m = 54$
    3. $d - m = 0$
    4. $d \times s = 21$
    5. $2 \times d + m = 84$

(continued)

22. Word Problems: Age Problems in the Future or Past, page 48:
    1. $m - 10 = 3(b - 10)$
    2. $e + 5 = 2(p + 5)$
    3. $m + 8 + p + 8 = 47$
    4. $j - 25 = 2(m - 25)$
    5. $p + 2 = m + 2 - 23$

23. Word Problems with Shapes and Dimensions, page 51:
    1. $L = W + 6$
    2. $P = 2L + 2W$
    3. $H = B + 5$
    4. $L = W + 2$
    5. $L = (W \times W) / W$

24. Word Problems: Coin Problems, page 54:
    1. 16 quarters, 2 dimes
    2. 6 quarters, 10 nickels
    3. 3 half-dollars, 4 dimes
    4. 4 quarters, 4 dimes, 5 nickels
    5. 15 pennies, 21 nickels

25. Mixture Problems with Nuts and Candy, page 56:
    1. 2 @ $1.50, 8 @ $1.25
    2. 4 @ $4.00, 6 @ $2.75
    3. 18 @ $.80, 2 @ $1.20
    4. 2 @ $.70, 8 @ $.50
    5. 8 @ $.40, 2 @ $1.00

26. Chemical Mixture Word Problems, page 59:
    1. 6 of 50%, 4 of 25%
    2. 9 of 70%
    3. 12 of 10%
    4. 12 of 15%, 18 of 20%
    5. 15 of 20%, 45 of 60%
    6. 8 of 50%, 16 of 20%
    7. 75 of 30%, 25 of 70%

27. "Can do a job in . . ." Word Problems, page 61:
    1. 1 hour $37\frac{1}{4}$ minutes
    2. $51\frac{2}{3}$ minutes
    3. 1 hour 12 minutes
    4. 43 minutes
    5. 40 minutes

28. Rate, Time, and Distance Problems, page 63:
    1. 8 hours
    2. 2 hours
    3. 6 hours
    4. 5 hours
    5. 11 hours, 15 minutes

29. Rate, Time, and Distance Problems: Alternating Speeds, page 64:
    1. 8 hours at 60 mph, 9 hours at 30 mph
    2. 4 hours at 30 mph, 6 hours at 20 mph
    3. 4 hours at 25 mph, 11 hours at 50 mph

30. Rate, Time, and Distance Problems: Water or Air Currents, page 66:
    1. 6 mph in still water, 3 mph current
    2. 6 mph in still water, 2 mph current
    3. 10.5 mph in still water, 3.5 mph current
    4. 55 mph in still air, 5 mph air current
    5. 450 mph in still air, 50 mph air current

31. Plotting Points on a Graph, page 69:
    1. From the center, 1 to the right, up 4
    2. From the center, 2 to the left, down 5
    3. From the center, 1 to the left, up 4
    4. From the center, down 3
    5. From the center, 4 to the right, down 1

(continued)

32. Finding Points from an Equation, page 71:
    1. (0,5), (1,6)
    2. (0,2), (1,4)
    3. (0,4), (1,8)
    4. (0,–6), (1,–1)
    5. (0,–2), (1,8)
    6. (0,0), (1,–2)
    7. (0,3), (1,0)

33. Finding the Distance Between Two Points, page 73:
    1. 4
    2. 2
    3. 4
    4. $\sqrt{17}$
    5. $\sqrt{104}$

34. Finding Slope, *y*-Intercept, and the Equation of a Line, page 75:
    1. $y = x + 5$
    2. $y = 6x$
    3. $y = 5x + 3$
    4. $y = -3x + 4$
    5. $y = 4x - 3$

35. Graphing Horizontal and Vertical Lines: $y = 2$, $x = 4$, page 77:
    1. Up 1, horizontal line
    2. Left 3, vertical line
    3. Vertical line through the origin (0,0)
    4. Right 2, vertical line
    5. Horizontal line through the origin (0,0)

36. Graphing Inequalities, page 79:
    1. Points (0,0), (1,2), shade left
    2. Points (0,1), (1,–2), shade right
    3. Points (0,–2), (1,1), shade right
    4. Points (0,–4), (1,–3), shade left
    5. Points (0,–3), (1,–1), shade right

37. Solving for *x*: Completing the Square, page 81:
    1. $x = -2 \pm \sqrt{2}$
    2. $x = -3 \pm \sqrt{7}$
    3. no solution
    4. $x = 1 \pm \sqrt{5}$
    5. $x = 4 \pm \sqrt{15}$

38. Solving for *x*: The Quadratic Formula, page 83:
    1. –2
    2. –3
    3. –1
    4. $1 \pm \sqrt{2}$
    5. 4
    6. 3 and 1

39. Solving for *x* with Fractions: Cross-Multiply and Divide, page 85:
    1. 3
    2. 9
    3. 0
    4. 45
    5. 6

40. Solving for *x*: Equations with Fractions, page 87:
    1. 6
    2. 35
    3. –5
    4. 1/2
    5. –14

41. Solving for *x*: Factoring Out, page 89:
    1. –3, –1
    2. 3, 2
    3. 0, –7
    4. 0, –1
    5. 3, 4

(continued)

42. Solving Gigantic Fractions, page 91
    1. $(1 + xy) / (xy^2 + y^3)$
    2. $(b - 2ab) / (3a^2 + 4ab)$
    3. $(4b^2 + a) / (ab^3 + ab)$
    4. $(y + 2x) / (1 - ax)$
    5. $(b^2c + b) / (2 + b^2c^3)$

43. Solving Two Equations: The Substitution Method, page 93:
    1. (2, 2)
    2. (25, 5)
    3. (–2, 7)
    4. (1, 5)
    5. (4, 1)

44. Solving Two Equations: Addition/ Elimination Method, page 96:
    1. (1, 1)
    2. (2, 1)
    3. (2, –2)
    4. (4, 3)
    5. (1, 9)

45. Is the Equation a Function?, page 98:
    1. Yes
    2. Yes
    3. No
    4. No
    5. Yes

46. Doing Function Problems as "Function Machines", page 100:
    1. 11
    2. 19
    3. 5
    4. 7
    5. 2

47. More "Function Machines", page 102:
    1. $a^2 + 2a + 5$
    2. 9

3. $a + b + 1$
4. $3 + y$
5. $g^2 + 2g + 1$

48. Domain and Range, page 104:
    1. $x = r$, $y \geq -2$
    2. $x = r$ except $x \neq -2$, $y = r$ except $y \neq 0$
    3. $x \geq -1$, $y \geq -1$
    4. $x = r$, $y \geq 4$
    5. $x = r$, $y \leq 1/4$

49. Variation Problems, page 106:
    1. $y = kmn$
    2. $y = ka \div bc$
    3. $y = kx \div z$
    4. $y = 64$
    5. $y = 4$

50. Symmetry and Degree, page 108:
    1. y-axis symmetry
    2. x-axis symmetry
    3. x-axis symmetry
    4. y-axis symmetry
    5. 7

51. Exponent Rules, page 110:
    1. y^8
    2. x^3
    3. $1 \div x^{14}$
    4. 1
    5. $x^4 + 2x^2y^2 + y^4$

52. Parabolas, page 112:
    1. Vertex (0, 0) – points (1, 1), (–1,1)
    2. Vertex (0,4) – points (1, 5), (–1,5)
    3. Vertex (0, 0) – points (1, –2), (–1, –2)
    4. Vertex (–2, 0) – points (–1, 1), (–3, 1)
    5. Vertex (0, 1) – points (–1, 6), (1, 6)

53. Parabolas: Completing the Square, page 114:
    1. Vertex (–2,–2) – points (–1,–1), (–3,–1),

(continued)

(0,2), (–4,2)

2. Vertex (1, –2) – points (0,–1), (2,–1), (–1,2), (3,2)

3. Vertex (-3,-3) – points (–2,–2), (–2,–4), (1,–1), (1,–5)

4. Vertex (2,2) – points (3,1), (3,3), (6,0), (6,4)

5. Vertex (–1,4) – points (0,5), (–2,5), (1,8), (–3,8)

54. Circles, page 117:
   1. Center (0, 0), radius = 2
   2. Center (2, 0), radius = 5
   3. Center (1, 2), radius = 3
   4. Center (–4, 5), radius = 4
   5. Center (–1, –3), radius = 4

55. Ellipses, page 120:
   1. Points at (±4,0), (0,±2)
   2. Points at (±5,0), (0,±6)
   3. Points at (±2, 0), (0,±1)
   4. Points at (±25,0), (0,±5)
   5. Points at (±4,0), (0,±2)

56. Hyperbolas, page 122:
   1. Box points (10,0), (–10,0), (0,8), (0,–8)
   2. Box points (1,0), (–1,0), (0,5), (0,–5)
   3. Box points (2,0), (–2,0), (0,1), (0,–1)
   4. Box points (1,0), (–1,0), (0,2), (0,–2)
   5. Box points (4,0), (–4,0), (0,2), (0,–2).
   Graph all answers from the x axis points.

57. Square Roots, page 124:
   1. $2\sqrt{5}$
   2. $3\sqrt{2}$
   3. 4
   4. 6
   5. $5\sqrt{2}$

58. Square Roots, a Chart, and Fraction Exponents, page 126:
   1. 3
   2. 5
   3. $3\sqrt{2}$
   4. $5\sqrt{2}$
   5. 3

59. More Square Roots and Fraction Exponents, page 128:
   1. 2
   2. 27
   3. 9
   4. 125
   5. 32

60. Getting Rid of Square Roots in Denominators, page 130:
   1. $\sqrt{3} \div 3$
   2. $2\sqrt[3]{3} \div 3$
   3. $[(\sqrt{3}) - 2] \div -1$
   4. $4\sqrt{5} \div 5$
   5. $\sqrt[3]{5}$

61. Adding, Subtracting, and Multiplying Square Roots, page 132:
   1. $7\sqrt{3}$
   2. $2\sqrt{5}$
   3. $4\sqrt{2}$
   4. 0
   5. $2\sqrt{6}$

62. Logarithm Rules, page 135:
   1. 2
   2. 0
   3. True
   4. True
   5. 64